Harold's Story

The tale of an RAF Armourer in WWII

Transcribed by Daphne Davison

Book Guild Publishing

First published in Great Britain in 2016 by

The Book Guild Ltd
9 Priory Business Park
Wistow Road, Kibworth
Leicestershire, LE8 0RX
Freephone: 0800 999 2982
www.bookguild.co.uk
Email: info@bookguild.co.uk
Twitter: @bookguild

Typeset in Garamond

Printed and bound in Great Britain by
CPI Group (UK) Ltd, Croydon, CR0 4YY

ISBN 978 1 910508 99 2

British Library Cataloguing in Publication Data.
A catalogue record for this book is available from the British Library.

In memory of my dear cousin
Harold Marsh
1922 – 2006

FOREWORD

I thought I would like to explain how *Harold's Story* came about.

I was born and spent my early years in Canterbury, where we lived at the start of the war and endured the frightful Blitz. My mother's family lived all around us in Whitstable and Faversham. My mother's mother, Granny Bootes, lived in Faversham, just a short bus ride from us, and I spent a lot of time there as Granny Bootes loved children and in particular her grandchildren. Faversham, and in particular where my grandmother and grandfather lived, was then a lovely place for small children to run around. There was a huge municipal recreational ground opposite my grandparent's house. This we called 'the rec' and beyond the rec were the railway shunting sidings where we could watch what was going on from an overhead walkway.

Granny Bootes's youngest daughter Gladys was usually around to join our games until she took up nursing and moved away to a teaching hospital in London. From there she would occasionally come home and bring one of her friends with her, and that is how we met the beautiful Una, who I thought impossibly glamorous. One day she borrowed Ted, my teddy bear, and returned him to me dressed in baby clothes. Then my cousin Harold Marsh began to appear, who I thought impossibly glamorous as well. He was the son of Granny Bootes's eldest daughter, May. He had a tan and wore RAF uniform and nobody was surprised when Harold and Una got married. They went to live in Essex, so we did not see very much of them.

Harold spent his later years in Wickford in Essex. His sight deteriorated as he got older and his son John got him to record on audio tape his war experiences, for something to do. We would try to see him if ever we were travelling that way and we were fascinated by the stories he had to tell, and he was such a lovely man as well. He lent us his tapes and as I played them I found them quite difficult to listen to. The quality of the tapes was poor and the narrative was peppered with 'Ums' and 'Ahs' and coughs etc. I discovered that his family had not listened to the tapes and I thought people would find it easier if the contents were written down. And there is always the risk that audio players would join all the other obsolete gadgetry.

The beginning of his story mostly concerned all the local things that happened. But what came as a complete surprise was his story of what happened to him in the Far East. I do not think that any one in the family was aware of the danger he had been in and what he had experienced. I could not wait sometimes typing up the next bit. As I typed I would send Harold's son John what I had completed and he would ring me to ask what happened next. Sadly Harold died on 12th February 2006. This is his story, told in his own voice. I have added nothing.

Daphne Davison

LIST OF PHOTOGRAPHS

CHAPTER ONE

I was born in Seasalter on the north coast of Kent on 18th March 1922 at my uncle and aunt's house. My uncle, Alf Waters, was the warden and caretaker of the Shaftesbury Homes for Children, and the house belonged to the Shaftesbury Homes. It was the children's summer camp. His wife Frances was my father's sister. The main home for the children was in London but the children used to come down to the holiday home in the summer holidays. The homes took in both boys and girls. As I remember there were about six large huts with beds.

My father had four brothers and two sisters. Aunt Frances, who helped her husband run the Shaftesbury Home at Seasalter, had three children, Vera, Dorothy and Billy. I had a total of seven cousins in all but I was more closely involved with Aunt Frances and her children.

My mother had four brothers. Willy, the eldest, had been killed near Roye in France in 1918 and another brother, Victor, had died as an infant of pneumonia. Another brother, Stanley, died about 20 years after the end of the First World War of tuberculosis which he contracted in the trenches, and another brother, Eddie, suffered all his life with breathing difficulties, having been gassed. My mother also had four sisters. The youngest was Gladys who arrived late on in my grandmother's life, and we were more or less brought up together, she being only two years older than me. I was frequently looked after by my grandmother as my mother suffered with a heart condition and was often unwell. It was because of her health that I remained an only child. My mother was christened Florence Grace May, but was always known as May, was truly a lovely lady and everybody loved her.

During the First World War my mother was employed, aged about 16, at the Munitions Factory on the Swale marshes outside Faversham, making bombs and artillery shells. One Sunday my grandmother was putting the joint into the oven of the kitchen range when the whole town was shaken by a tremendous explosion as the factory blew up, with tremendous loss of life. I have to credit the fact that I am here with my son and grandchildren to the policy of the factory not employing women and girls on a Sunday. When I was about six my mother was taken seriously ill and I was sent to live with my Granny Bootes in Faversham for several months, and I had to go to school there, and I hated it.

For several Christmases the entire family on my father's side hired a coach (we called it a charabanc) and went over to Deal where we had relatives who ran a boarding house and we all celebrated Christmas together. There was not enough room for all of us to sleep in beds and some of the children slept in beds made up on the floor. All my uncles and boy cousins and myself shared two bedrooms and my aunts and girl cousins all slept together in other bedrooms. On Christmas Day all the men and boys were sent out while the ladies cooked the Christmas dinner.

One Christmas morning we were walking along the sea front and we were approached by two small children who looked very poor. They asked us if we could give them some pennies and if we did they would sing us a comic song. We said we would give them some pennies but they must sing their song first. They said they could not sing with us looking at them so they faced the other way. To tease them a little we hopped into a shop doorway. When they turned back again they thought we had run away but we burst out on them, laughing. This is the song they sang:

> The Corporation dung cart was loaded to the brim,
> The driver overbalanced and found he couldn't swim,
> So he sank to the bottom, like a little stone
> And all the little fishes sang to him,
> This is no place like home.

One of my uncles took the two children back to their home and invited their parents to come back with us to share our Christmas and somehow we fitted them in with all the rest of us and they were even found some Christmas presents. Some other Christmases we had, my parents, aunts and uncles saved for us all to have a big party. My father worked then in a small factory making chocolates and the man who owned the factory also owned a hall and he would let us have the hall for our family party. All my cousins and friends would come, including my Aunt Gladys, who was only a year or two older than me, and we all had a lovely time.

Harold's parents Henry and May Marsh at 8 Norfolk Street, Whitstable.

My father fought as a soldier in the First World War and suffered several serious and incapacitating injuries. He was shot in the hip and in both feet. The bullet entered my father's hip with a small entry wound to the front but as bullets are designed to spiral and twist, left a very large exit wound and smashed his pelvis. He was shot through both feet, with an entry wound on his right side and the bullet exited on his left side. The only way that his wounds could be dealt with at that time was to fuse his hip and leg together that he could not bend his leg. He suffered greatly over the years yet he always seemed cheerful and happy. He was taken prisoner by the Germans and spent some considerable time in captivity. Some soldiers in the trenches were driven mad or insane by the appalling conditions and were sent home. Other soldiers observing this would pretend to go mad in order to get sent home and they would be closely watched. Some would do it so well and for so long that they actually went mad.

The earliest place that I remember was 8 Norfolk Street, Whitstable. My grandmother Marsh lived round the corner in Suffolk Street, and both were just a short distance from the sea. Both Norfolk Street and Suffolk Street led into the main street running through Whitstable. The gardens of the houses in the main street backed onto some of the gardens in Norfolk Street. Alleyways ran between the houses giving access to the back gardens. My particular friends all lived round about and we would gather down at the corner where there was a gas lamp. There was a timber yard on one corner and stables on the other. My particular friends were Bobby Ashcroft and his sister Agnes, Jack Warner, Stevie Wansall and Teddy Levy. Mona and Eveline Austin, two girls who lived nearby, would join us as well.

We played the usual games that children then would play. We would play cricket using the lamp post as a wicket. And we would play with tops and hoops. The girls had wooden hoops and the boys had metal hoops. And we would play hide and seek and run races round the two streets and the alleyways. We would also play leapfrog, and another game we had was one of us would lean forward against a wall and see how many other children could sit on his back until he collapsed. We would all take turns in doing this.

My father was very clever at making toys and other

*Costumes made by Harold's father, Henry Marsh for
the Whitstable Carnival.*

*Harold as a penny collecting box and his aunt Gladys as a butterfly at the
Whitstable Carnival.*

Harold with his parents.

things to keep us children amused. Also he had infinite patience. One Christmas someone gave me a box containing six jigsaw puzzles all jumbled up together. There were no pictures to guide me and all the puzzles seemed to be similar in background and to be of sea and boats. My father took the puzzles and sat down and sorted them out for me. It took him the whole of one Sunday. He would always make costumes for us for the Whitstable annual carnival. One year he made me a costume as a penny. He cut out two circles in plywood with a frame inside so that I could get inside it and then he painted it as how the front and reverse of a penny would be. He then made a frame to go over my head to act as a collecting box in aid of the cottage hospital, with a picture of the hospital and an ambulance painted on it. I won first prize for that. Aunt Gladys took part, dressed as a butterfly; my dad made the wings. Gladys was meant to flap her arms to work the wings but she thought that was silly and refused to do it! There used to be a comic at that time called *Bruno* and they would supply animal heads on request. My father got a bear's head and a horse's head from them and made the costumes for another of the Whitstable carnivals. The horse's head became part of a pantomime horse. My father made me a toy fort with a drawbridge that could be let up and down and relatives would give me lead soldiers for birthday and Christmas presents. He also put wheels on a wooden box with an elementary steering device that gave my friends and me hours of amusement rattling around the alleyways.

Living by the seaside, of course, we boys joined the Sea Scouts and the ordinary Scouts as well, and we would all go off to camp in the summer. I found that when I tried cycling with my backpack full of the things I needed for camp, I kept falling off with the weight of it. My father spent a great deal of time alongside me, going round and round the garden paths on my bicycle, but it was no good: as soon as he stopped helping I would fall off. So he hired a small bus and took me and my friends to the camp. Older friends who had already left school and were working would cycle over to see us in the evenings. One day they treated us to a monster portion of fish and chips which they bought on the way. However, when they opened up the newspaper all the fish and chips had turned into one big soggy mass. We still ate it though. Once we went to a Scout camp that was held at Chilham Castle, near Canterbury. There were scores of us and the grounds were covered in the small two-sleeper tents. There was a deer park in the grounds which we all thought fascinating. At night we would all sing songs around a camp fire, in traditional manner. Another time I went to a summer Scout camp which was by some fields where the farmer was harvesting the corn, and he asked if we would help catch the rabbits and hares as they ran out of the corn as it was being cut. We were not very good at it and most of them got away but I was given a hare to take home. My mother said that hares did not taste very good but she cooked a leg just for me and I thought it was just lovely.

At the Silver Jubilee celebrations for King George and Queen Mary a huge bonfire was built at the top of the hill behind where we lived. The bonfire site overlooked the whole of Whitstable and the Boy Scouts volunteered to guard it to stop anybody trying to light it before the appropriate time. My friend Billy and I took our small tent up to the top of the hill and put it up beside the huge bonfire but some boys coming by said they had heard some people say they were going to come and set fire to it, which Billy and I thought was rather alarming, and when it got dark we took down our tent and ran down to my home and put it up there on the lawn. We told ourselves that we could watch perfectly well from there and anyway, we told ourselves, if someone did set fire to it we might be blamed for it. However, some of the bigger Scouts came along as it got dark and set up their

Cousin's birthday party at Whitstable. Early 1930s. Harold seated at front with his toy monkey. His mother is kneeling behind him. Harold's cousin Peter – the birthday boy – is seated on Granny Bootes' lap, aunt Gladys stands behind.

tents and guarded it till the morning. Later the following day there were big parades for the Silver Jubilee and the Scouts were given Silver Jubilee medals and also another medal for having guarded the bonfire. My friend Billy and I had the cheek to accept one as well!

When I was about ten my father bought a piece of ground on the edge of Whitstable and had a bungalow built. My mother and I used to go up there every day to watch the progress of the building and to see how many more bricks had been laid. At the bottom end of the garden there was a large natural pond. At that time the piece of ground round the pond, which was owned by another man, was covered with hawthorn bushes. My father, to the best of his abilities, helped this man clear the bushes away and it looked very nice.

I would sit in a tree at the bottom of the garden with an airgun and shoot at the newts in the pond as they rose to the surface. The newts never came to any harm as the surface of the water dissipated the force of the pellets, and I was a rotten shot anyway. Of course the newts, having been disturbed, would settle at the bottom of the pond until I went away. One day, up in the tree, I broke open the air rifle to reload it and did not fasten it shut properly, and when I fired it, it flew back, hitting me on the nose and being startled, I fell out of the tree. I still have the scars to this day. That was one up to the newts. On another occasion I fired at a sparrow in the hedge in front of the house. I don't think I hurt it but it did lose a few feathers as it flew away and I was so ashamed of what I had done I did not use the air rifle ever again. We were then living on the edge of the town in our new bungalow and in the summer I would go out with my friends into the fields and woods around us and play all day. We would take a bottle of water with us and some sandwiches.

I would also go over to Seasalter to see my aunt Frances and play with my cousin Vera. And then my uncle Alf moved even further out into the marshes and set up a chicken farm. He built some large huts to house the chickens and I remember buying a hammer with my pocket money to help him. Whether I was any help at all, I rather doubt, but my uncle appreciated that I did try. My cousins and I would sail small model boats in the dykes and ditches and we would go fishing with a bit of bread on a bent pin on a piece of string. Amazingly we did catch one or two fish, but not many.

My granny Bootes lived in Faversham, which is Shepherd Neame country, and she would go hop picking every summer. It was very hard work but times were hard and people did it to make a little extra money. My gran would start picking hops at 7.30 in the morning but first they had a 3 mile walk to get to the hop field. The hop fields were quite spectacular before the pickers started on them. The hop bines were strung up on wires about 10 foot high, making green leafy tunnels beneath. The bines had to be pulled down to be picked and my gran, who was a diminutive lady, seemed to have the knack of getting them down with what seemed like no difficulty at all. The hops were then picked off the bines by hand into a bushel basket, and the pickers were paid by the basket. When the bine was pulled down it would invariably fall on the picker complete with dust, sulphur powder which had been put on the bines, twigs and insects, and if it had rained or there had been a heavy dew, a shower of water as well. Then the picker would pull the bine across their lap, and sitting on a wooded stool or box, work their way through it, picking off all the hops. It was very hard work.

My gran was a hard worker and could scratch the hops off (as they called it) among the fastest, but they were only paid about 4 pence a bushel. One year the pickers decided that they were not being paid enough and went on strike and the field owners gave in and increased their pay to 6 pence a bushel, and they felt they had won a big victory.

Four times a day the tally man would come round and all the hops would be tipped into a large basket with markers at the end of the row, and the tally man would measure how far up the hops came and mark the picker's card so that the money could be claimed at the end of the hop picking. The hops in the basket would be tipped into a large sack by a couple of the farm workers and then a horse and cart would come round to pick up the sacks.

People from the East End of London would come down in the summer for the hop picking. They would call it their summer holiday. The farmer provided wooden huts for them. Inside there were concrete slabs and the Londoners would put straw on these and sleep on them. I tried it for one night and I don't think I have ever passed such an uncomfortable night.

Sometimes I would spend part of my summer holidays at my gran's in Faversham with my aunt Gladys for company. We would get up later and then walk over to the hop field to find my grandmother. When I got older I would sometimes cycle over from Whitstable to spend the day with Gran and Gladys in the hop field. My gran would say we would have to pick a few baskets of hops and then we could play or go home, but a lot of children would have to pick hops all day. Sometimes when a bine was too difficult to pull down both Gladys and I would swing on it and then it would come down with a rush and bury us both. That was rather unpleasant as the bine was heavy and the hop leaves were very scratchy and we would be covered in dust and insects and insect powder.

During the day a sweet man would do the rounds of the hop fields with a tray of sweets. He would make a cone from newspaper and fill the cone up for us for a halfpenny or whatever. The day's picking would start with the tally man blowing a horn at half past seven, and then he would blow it again at twelve for us to have our midday meal, and he would blow it again at five in the afternoon for us to finish. The hops would stain our hands black and we would eat our midday meal holding the sandwiches between pieces of newspaper.

My grandmother would go cherry picking as well as hop picking and I liked that better as I was very fond of cherries. The pickers were allowed to bring a small quantity back home. It is amazing to think of my grandmother cherry picking as she was so tiny and she had to cope with the huge ladders that they used then.

I had saved up as a boy to get my bicycle but mostly we went everywhere then by bus. When my mother and father and I used to visit my grandmother together in Faversham we would go by bus. I don't remember that we had bus stops then as we would wait indoors for the bus as we lived on the bus route, and as soon as we saw the bus coming we would dash out and stop it. My grandmother and grandfather lived next door to a fish and chip shop, in East Street, which I thought was quite wonderful.

My grandfather worked for Faversham Town Council. Sometimes he would have to go round and light the gas street lamps if the regular man was away for some reason. He would have a long pole with a light on the top of it to light the lamps. My grandfather kept rabbits in hutches in the small back garden and he would go down into the back garden every night to cover the rabbits over for the night and he would take a lighted candle with him to see to lock the back gate. One time I was there I had been given a torch as a present so he used the torch to light his way and much to Gladys's and my amusement when he got back into the kitchen we found him trying to blow the torch out, as he was so used to blowing out his candle. My grandparents rented their house as most people did in those days. Of course it did not have a bathroom. Small children would be bathed in the kitchen sink. Kitchen sinks were bigger in those days, as the weekly washing would be done in the sink. As we got bigger we would bath in a tin bath, and the bigger you got the nearer your knees got to your chin. Water would be heated up in kettles and pots and pans on the kitchen range. My gran's house had an outside toilet and as it did not have a flushing cistern we had to take a bucket of water out to wash it down. When my parents had their new bungalow built it had only an Elsan toilet which would be emptied as necessary into a hole dug in the garden.

Most people lived in rented houses and it would depend on the landlord, who was usually the owner, as to what condition the house would be in. People accepted that then because that was how life was.

Winters were colder then and we would have snow most years and most of the boys in Whitstable, as it seemed to me then, would come to the hill at the back of us with their toboggans and tin trays to slide noisily down the hill.

Once we had a whale beach itself on the seashore. Gladys and I would go down to the beach quite often to play and one time we were chasing each other and I jumped over a breakwater only to find deep water the other side and as I splashed about Gladys, thinking I was drowning, jumped in to rescue me. We splashed about for a bit until we realised that if we stood up the water only came to our knees. We still got into trouble when we got home.

When I left school I was apprenticed to an electrician. Feeling very grown up I went and bought myself five cigarettes which I smoked and then felt very ill. My boss asked what was wrong and then he said, 'You've been smoking,' and gave me a cuff round the ears.

Chapter Two

When I was about sixteen and a half I thought I would like to go into the navy. My father talked me out of this and advised me to try to join the RAF (a couple of years into the war I was very pleased that he did this). I applied to the RAF recruitment office and was told that I was too old for the boys' service and that I would have to wait until I was seventeen and a quarter.

Eventually a letter arrived telling me to report to the Air Ministry on 19th June 1939. My mother and gran decided they wanted to come with me as they had not been to London for a long time, so we all went off together. I had to go into a large hall where there were many other young men and I was given a Maths test and then a medical and other tests. I was there for the best part of the day and then I was told I had passed. I rushed outside and quickly told my mother and gran, and then we all had to line up and be marched off to the nearest underground station. I didn't let on to the others that my mum and gran were there.

We were taken to West Drayton in Middlesex. Here at West Drayton we were introduced to the Royal Air Force. The next morning we were given breakfast which was very good and at lunch time we were given ice cream and I began to think that this was definitely the life for me. We had lots of forms to fill in and I swore to serve my King and Country, and I was given my service number 648355 which became part of my life for the next six years or so, as familiar to me as my own name. I finished my first day in the RAF peeling potatoes in the cookhouse and then picking up rubbish around the camp.

The following day we were all loaded into lorries and taken to Uxbridge where we were accommodated in huge barracks blocks which were situated around a vast parade ground. Everything was on a huge scale: the cookhouse, the canteen and the drill hall where we queued to collect our pay on pay day. We were all issued with our kit. There seemed to be lots of it. Two uniforms (and underwear) shirts, a greatcoat, two hats, a ceremonial peaked cap and a Glengarry, two kitbags, all sorts of webbing, a 'housewife' which was a sewing kit for running repairs, a button stick and boots. We were then sent to the Armoury to collect our rifle and bayonet. The rifle seemed very heavy. We were then sent off to the PE instructor. He was an intimidating and enormous man with a full head of hair which he had cut to half an inch all over. He shouted at us that he was Corporal Clayton, better known as 'Bastard' Clayton, and we were about to find out why. However, before we could discover this he was suddenly demoted, losing his stripes and posted somewhere else, much to our relief. We all had to visit the barbers, much to the grief of some of the men who were proud of their pretty wavy locks. We were given metal discs to pay for our haircuts and we all came out with the regulation short back and sides and a half inch all over.

Uxbridge, the camp where we were, was known to be

the smartest and most strict RAF camp in the country, and shortly after we arrived there a company from the camp was chosen to be the ceremonial guard for the King and Queen on their return from a royal visit to Canada.

After we had had our inoculations for all number of diseases we were all marched down to a local school where we had to sit a fairly rigorous maths exam to determine our aptitude for various trades in the RAF. Some of the trades on offer were engineer, wireless operator and armourer, among others. Those who did not pass were assigned to GD, or General Duties. I passed, much to my surprise, and I chose to become an armourer. The ones who chose to become wireless operators drove us all mad in our billet learning the Morse Code shouting DAR DAR DIT DAR at each other into the small hours of the night.

After all of us had shaken down then RAF life began in earnest. We had parade ground inspections, drill and PE, both outside on the parade ground and in the drill hall. I quite liked the PE outdoors on the parade ground but was not too sure about the indoors PE, as we were expected to exercise with the large wooden vaulting horses. We were all stiff at first but that soon wore off.

We were given pictures of how our beds and kit should be laid out for inspection and we soon got the hang of it. We were expected to keep our rifles spotlessly clean and we were given a 'pull through' to use on it. The rifles were inspected regularly by the officers during parade ground drill.

We had to keep our billet spotless as well. The floor was waxed and then had a heavy bumper pulled over it until the floor shone like a mirror. The stove in the centre of the billet was polished until that shone also. In the evenings we had to polish our brass buttons and buckles. We also had to do kitchen fatigues and guard duties. When we were on guard duty we would be on duty for 24 hours, two hours on, four hours off, and during that time we would not get undressed. The only thing we took off was our cap.

When we were on guard duty we would have to parade outside the guard house at half past three in the afternoon and we would be inspected by an orderly officer. One day during guard inspection the orderly officer told the man standing next to me to hand over his rifle for inspection, which he did. He was then arrested and spent the night in the cells, as he was told that he should never hand his rifle over for any reason whatsoever. I was lucky, as I would have done the same myself.

Towards the end of the ten weeks we were in training I had a 48-hour pass and went home to Whitstable. If you had a pass you had to report to the guard house with your pass before leaving in order to be signed out. We had to march down a corridor to where the Service Police were sitting. There were mirrors around the walls and if it was discovered you had so much as a piece of cotton on the back of your tunic you were not allowed to remove it there and you had to march back to your barrack block to do it.

When I got home I was told my parents were at the cinema so I went along and persuaded the usherette to let me go in. I knew where they would be sitting because of my father's legs. I got round my father and my mother stood

Harold in his RAF uniform.

up to let me pass, which I did with my back to her. She only realised I was sitting next to her when the lights came back on.

The last days of basic training passed and we had our passing out parades. If recruits did not come up to the standard required then they would have to stay for another ten weeks. I passed and felt very proud, and also I felt very fit. It had been hard, very hard, but I had to admit that I had enjoyed it.

After my initial training I was posted to Shrewsbury. I was there on 3rd September 1939 when war was declared. Discipline at Shrewsbury was not as strict as it had been at basic training camp and the men that had been there for a while had got sloppy with the drill. We still had to do guard duties but we just marched about without paying much attention. Daily Routine Orders (DROs) were issued but one particular day I did not read that all servicemen on guard duty were to report to the square for rifle drill. I did my guard duty, then found out what Form 252 was for. It was a charge sheet. I was taken up before the Commanding Officer and got confined to barracks for seven days. That meant you could not leave the barracks and you had to report to the guard room where you were given fatigues to do. I spent the evenings that week cleaning windows.

After that my posting came for me to commence the armoury course in Pembrey in South Wales so I packed my kitbag and was off again. All this travelling came as a novelty to me, as in the 1930s people just did not travel about. As I remember it, Margate was the furthest away that I had travelled away from home as a child.

The camp in South Wales was a new one and we were the first lot of RAF men to be billeted there. It was all wooden huts, but very comfortable and we were regarded as a novelty by the local people and when we went down into the village on the Sunday a lot of us were invited into the people's homes and shared their Sunday dinner with them. Me and my friends were invited into the home of the village parson. We still had to do guard duty in the camp here but it was nothing like Uxbridge, we just had to patrol round the billets and the main road. There was a small river which flowed through part of the camp and one night when I went to relieve one of the men on guard I couldn't find him, so I went back and reported to the Corporal in the guard room and everyone was turned out to search for him. We found him in the river looking for his tin hat. There was a path at the side of the river and they both looked the same in the moonlight and he had chosen the wrong one to walk on and gone into the river.

The armoury course that I was on was a six-month course up until the outbreak of the war, but now there was a greater sense of urgency and the course became more intensive, designed to turn us out fully competent in three months. We were given instruction in all different types of bombs and all different types of guns including revolvers and rifles. When we eventually passed out, none of us had passed out with very high colours. We all passed out as Aircraftsman, Second Class, none of us passed out as AC1. After this, it was realised there was too much to take in on the course in three months, so the men were divided into two groups, and half were taught the armoury for fighter plane guns and the other half were taught the armoury required by bomber planes. I was classified as Armourer General, which is what I had been taught, but the new lot would be known as Armourer Guns or Armourer Bomb. The bullets for fighter planes came in three different types, one general, one armour-piercing and one incendiary, and each one came in different colours, the same with the bombs. We had to learn about the guns used in planes; each one had about 20 different parts, some of them moveable parts which if installed incorrectly would jam the gun. We had to learn the names of all these parts.

We had to go onto the rifle range and learn to use rifles and machine guns. We had done a bit of this at Uxbridge but there was much more of it here in Pembrey. I have to say at this point that all the men I served with, then and throughout the war, we all got on well with each other and there were never any disputes or arguments. We all realised we were in the same boat and we had to get on with it. After we had passed our exams it was Christmas time. I was posted to No. 3 Squadron stationed at Manston in Kent. The train to Manston passed through the station in Whitstable so I got off the train at Whitstable, and leaving my kitbag in the booking office I went home for a couple of hours. I then took the train on to Margate and rang through to the RTO, the Road Transport Office and asked to be picked up from the station as it was snowing heavily. They said the snow was too deep to send out transport and I would have to walk to the camp. I took my washbag out of my kit and leaving my kitbag at the station set out on foot. The base at Manston is on a bleak, flat piece of countryside surrounded by cabbage fields and I kept falling into snowdrifts in the ditches. I went into the guard room and reported to the Service Policeman and he laughed and told me that No. 3 Squadron had been posted on two weeks before. He gave me a bed for the night and I planned to walk back to the railway station in the morning to collect my kit. I explained what I was doing to the Orderly Room Officer and I mentioned that my home was in Whitstable close by, and he gave me a 48-hour pass, so I was at home with my mum and dad at the begining of the new year of 1940.

I caught up with No. 3 Squadron in Croydon, which was then the main airport for London. I particularly remember being struck by how enormous all the installation buildings seemed. The main hangar was so big that several houses could have been put inside it. I reported to the orderly room

Harold with 3 squadron in France (third from left, middle row).

officer who took me over to the No. 3 Squadron hangar, where I was introduced to the men with whom I would be spending the next few years. I was taken to stores and issued with my kit, which included my bed and bedding. I was given two small, low trestles and three planks, two sacks, one small and one larger and some blankets, and then I was directed where to fill the sacks up with straw, and this was my bed! It was bitterly cold and we put up our beds in the small brick-built workshops alongside the main hangar where we froze overnight. The squadron consisted of Hurricanes and I was given a Hurricane to maintain.

We had been there only a week and we were then posted on to Kenley, which was to become a Battle of Britain airfield as the war progressed. Kenley was a proper Air Force base with brick-built billets and at last we had proper beds! We became used to working a proper structured day. We had to start our day with a full inspection of our plane and then go and sign a form, Form 700 as I remember, to say the inspection had been properly conducted; and heaven help you then if anything went wrong. I can't remember how many planes there were at that point, but quite a few. There were always two or three planes ready on standby and when they were sent off on patrol another two or three would take their place. Obviously when there was a 'scramble' most of the planes would take off and we would have to meet the planes on their return. We would inspect them to see if they had fired any of their guns and if so there was a panic to get them rearmed as soon as possible. The guns along the front edge of the wings had patches over them and you could see immediately if the patches were missing and that the guns had been used. We got rearming down to a fine art with an armourer on each wing, with an assistant on the ground, and the planes could be refuelled and turned around ready to take off again in seven or eight minutes. We worked three shifts throughout the day and night and it was hard work and very tiring. When the planes were not involved in combat we would give them a good overhaul.

We would go to the NAAFI for a bit of relaxation in the evening and have a game of darts and what we called a 'cup of tea and a wad': rock cakes, and they really seemed like rock. Sometimes we would get on the train to Croydon and go to the cinema. On the way back if we had any money we would get a taxi back to the barracks so we did not have to climb up the steep hill, and what a steep hill that was. Some of the men would go off for the evening in the pub and spend all their money and then have to climb that hill back. I did not smoke or drink in those days – I was a good boy!

We were issued with secondhand greatcoats to work in and one of the lads decided to clean his coat up as they were always coming into contact with oil so he washed it out in petrol then hung it up to dry outside his window. One of the other lads flicked his cigarette out the window and the coat went up in flames. I'm afraid we all laughed.

One morning we were told to pack up all our equipment and stores as we would be on the move in a few days' time. We were not told where. A couple of days after that a couple of air transport planes came in. They were the biggest planes that we had ever seen at that time. I was fascinated by the huge wheels of the planes; they were taller than me when I stood besides them. We were told to load up the planes and, except for ten of us, were told to get on board. It seems strange to relate that up to that point none of us had been up in a plane. Another plane then came on to the field and we were told to get on board with the Air Officer Commanding. This third plane was a German plane with three guns, a Messerschmidt, and was very strange; it looked as though it was made of corrugated iron. We were then told that we were going to Merville in France. At Merville we were billetted in Nissen huts in a field.

We unpacked our kit and tried to make the huts as comfortable as possible. We were bombed a couple of times and lost a couple of planes but our chief enemy there was boredom as there was nothing to do when we were off duty. There was a very small village nearby with one very small cafe and when we ventured there we were accused of stealing the teaspoons! We were not there for very long when the AOC had us gather on the airfield and told us the Germans were advancing on us and we would have to evacuate immediately. It was important that the planes be got away as soon as possible as both planes and air crew were desperately needed in England. We did not have time to pack much, just bare essentials, before a lorry arrived to take us away. The lorry driver got lost and when we came to a fork in the road, he decided to take one turning. Fortunately for us an army despatch rider drove up and told us the Germans were 4 or 5 miles in front of us, and to go back. We had a lucky escape from either being killed or taken prisoner. We managed to make it back to Boulogne where we had a rough night in shelters as the Germans were bombing the ports.

In the morning an officer told us to help unload a ship in the harbour which was full of stores and ammunition and as it was that ship we should be returning on the quicker it was unloaded the quicker we would be got away. I do not think there was a ship that was emptied as fast as that one and we got away that morning back to England and then back to Kenley. Shortly after our arrival back at Kenley I was promoted to AC1, I was going up in the world.

CHAPTER THREE

More men were being drafted into the forces all this time and assimilated into the existing companies and our squadron was split into three, and 232 Squadron and I were posted to Montrose in Scotland just before Christmas 1941. It was bitterly cold and the billets were makeshift affairs, and we were billeted in farm buildings. In what passed for our dining area there was a partition where you could see the cows the other side. It had snowed, and although we had proper beds you could see the moon through holes in the roof and we all slept in our clothes. When we went to breakfast we just put on our hats.

After a short while the authorities commandeered a roadhouse to accommodate us. It had a dance floor where we and all the conscripts put up their beds, and as time passed and more and more men arrived to join our squadron the dance floor resembled one huge bed with only just enough room to pass between the beds. One of my friends became friendly with a local girl and one day he told me that his girlfriend, Wendy, had a girlfriend who also wanted a boyfriend and was I interested? I said I was and the next evening we set off to meet them where they worked, which we were told was a large house owned by some wealthy people. Wendy worked there as a cook and her friend worked there as a maid. We found the house and were rather intimidated as it was a huge place. Where Wendy worked, the kitchen, was a massive cavernous room in the basement, but we were made welcome and given some plates of hot food which we thought was wonderful. The only problem was that the girls were not supposed to bring friends into the house and if a member of the family should come downstairs into the kitchen, we had to hide in a large wall-cupboard.

Shortly after this my girlfriend and I arranged to go to the cinema one evening, in Montrose. Just as we got to the cinema, one of my mates came running up and asked me to give him a hand with Taffy as he was dead drunk and asleep in someone's garden. We went down a side alley and found him lying in the garden of a small house. We shook him and shook him but he would not wake up. Every time we stood him up he fell down again, so we gave him up as a bad job and I went and rejoined my young lady and we went to the cinema. When I got back to our billet I found, much to my amazement, that Taffy had made it back, God knows how, and he was standing in the middle of the room in his greatcoat, still with his eyes shut, with his hands in his pockets, and four men trying to get him undressed.

The cinema in Montrose was at the back of a row of shops with a carpeted passageway leading down to it, with a bar on one side of the passageway and a restaurant on the other. This restaurant had a canary in a cage which was on a stand. One day when I got back to our billet I found the canary, complete with stand, in the middle of our room. One of the men had taken it as a bet, and claimed he had done it with nobody noticing. Anyway, he took it back the next morning and handed it back to its owner and explained he had done it for a bet, and fortunately the man just laughed.

We were still having men arriving to join our squadron and the squadron was once again divided, into A and B Flight. The company I was in were moved to another billet which was inside the town of Montrose itself and was some sort of small castle by the river. There were four of us allocated to a bedroom and the room had a wash hand basin and was heated! Unheard-of luxury to us.

It was still very cold weather with about a foot or so of snow on the ground so there was no flying. Then one morning the Flight Commander demonstrated that we could fly and went up in one of the planes. He took off all right and circled the field a couple of times, but when he landed the snow clogged up the wheels and the plane did a couple of somersaults. Fortunately the officer was not injured.

We were enjoying ourselves in Montrose, but as usual all good things have to come to an end and we were told one morning to pack up our kit and we were to be stationed at Wick. We all looked at each other, as none of us had heard of Wick. We were taken to the station by lorry and then we were put on the train for the north of Scotland. From the train windows all we could see were hills and mountains covered in snow. We wondered at first why the train kept stopping and then we realised that people were getting off in the middle of nowhere and trudging off into the distance in the snow, and the train was also stopping to pick up people as well.

When we got to Wick we found we were billeted again in Nissen huts. The roofs of the Nissen huts were white and all the pathways were white and the roof of the cookhouse was white, and it did not take us long to realise that this was caused by seagull droppings. It was difficult to make a trip anywhere outside without being 'bombed'. The seagulls became such an irritation that some of the lads would tie a piece of meat to both ends of a piece of string and toss it in the air and the gulls were so greedy that they would fly off with two seagulls joined together with a piece of string. Another trick was to tie a piece of meat on a piece of string with a blown-up paper bag on the other, and you would see gulls flying around towing a paper bag. There was not a lot to do there apart from the NAAFI. We would sometimes go to the fish and chip shop in Wick; there was a 'proper' restaurant downstairs which we christened the Hell Hole, but of course the fish was lovely as it was all so fresh. There was also a cinema of sorts.

If we had a leave pass it was quite a performance to get down south. From Wick to Inverness the railway was single track and there would only be one train a day, so we would sleep on the train. As the train got further south it would slowly fill up until it was a mass of bodies and kitbags which you would have to climb over if you wanted to go to the toilet. It got so that you wouldn't bother. We all grumbled about our posting in Wick and the boredom and monotony of it all but we did not know what was to come. We were told to pack up as we were again on the move … to the Shetland Islands! At about that time the Germans had invaded and occupied the Channel Islands and the Government were worried that they might do the same to the Shetland Islands so here we were, off again.

We took off in a gale, and looking out of the windows of the plane we could see nothing except mist and rain. Anyway we landed safely at Sumburgh Head with nothing to greet us except sheep and birds. It was a wonderful place for birdwatching if you liked that sort of thing. Needless to say, there had been no preparations for our arrival and we found that four of us had to share a bell tent, much to our disgust. It was very cold and although the tent had a wooden floor, that was all, not even anything to sit on. If the Germans had invaded we did not even have a pea shooter to fire at them. The only happy ones were those who smoked, as they were issued with 60 cigarettes a week free of charge, and we had a rum ration as well because of the cold. So what did Harold do? Of course he took up smoking.

We had nothing much to do. We were given every third day off to do our washing and other personal chores. All our stores were delivered in wooden crates and we made ourselves beds from the crates which got us up off the floor and away from the draughts, and we made ourselves a locker each to put by our beds. This made life a little more tolerable as well as giving us something to do. Three planes would take off together on patrol but never fired their armament, so we didn't get particularly dirty.

Strange to say, for want of anything to do we did go birdwatching and found it very interesting. There were lots of beautiful birds to see on the cliff, puffins and so on. We climbed up round Sumburgh Head and we could see another smaller bay round the other side. Our Sergeant organised us making a raft, which by the time we finished making it was a huge great heavy thing, and we launched it into the bay in order to go and investigate the other bay we had seen round the other side of the Head but we struggled to get it out – the current proved too strong for us. It was the North Atlantic current of course. We were taken by lorry to the main town in Shetland, Lerwick, as we had been told there was a cinema there. When we eventually found it, it seemed to be in someone's front room and anyway it was too late by then and we had to get back on the lorry and return to the camp. Although we grumbled a lot about where we were, we were quite aware we were better off than most of the people in the south who were being bombed. At least we could sleep easy on our home-made beds. Some of the lads did attempt to get home on leave but it was difficult as they had to get to Lerwick and wait for a boat to take them to Aberdeen and then get the train from there. If the weather was rough the boats did not leave. The ones that did go off on leave usually got back looking quite green with seasickness.

Then, of course, we were told we were on the move again. We fantasised about going somewhere where we would be given beds with springs! We went by lorry to Lerwick and then by ship to Wick. There were lorries waiting for us and insead of our old billets we were taken about eight or so miles down the road to a place called Skitten which was so terrible and bleak we wished we were back in the Shetlands. It was completely barren, not a sheep or bird to be seen.

We went into the huts and found there was no furniture. No beds, only 'biscuits' lying on the floor. The officers also were not pleased as they had to share accommodations with us and we all had to eat together. When we picked up the biscuits from the floor the next morning they were soaking wet on the underside where the heat from our bodies had drawn the damp up from the ground. We complained to our CO and he promised to get some beds for us, and later in the day a lorry drove up, loaded not with beds, but tables! So we slept on tables. Then we all got diarrhoea. We were issued with buckets and, of course, we were all sleeping on tables and having to get down to the floor from the table in the night and find a bucket was not something that even now I want to think about. We had chemical Elsan earth closets which were full to overflowing. I did not envy the poor so-and-so who had to clear them out.

I got severe toothache while there, and we had no medical staff except for a medical orderly who had no training. He arranged for an ambulance to pick me up at midday and take me to Wick for treatment. When the ambulance arrived I got in it and the driver got out and disappeared. I sat there for two hours and the driver never came, but luckily my toothache disappeared so I got out of the ambulance and carried on with my work and nothing more was said about it. Everyone there was complaining about the conditions. The officers did not like having to share accommodations with us, and not having a bar and other comforts they expected to have. Obviously the CO was putting in complaints to the authorities. I thought of writing to Hitler and asking him to come and bomb the place. I am sure if he had seen how we were living he would have sent us his condolences. Fortunately we were not there very long before we were sent further south to an established base at Newcastle. This was a proper camp with brick-built billets and proper accommodations.

The first day we were there the Station Officer came into our billet and told us to put on our best uniforms and to parade on the square. We were told that we had to parade every morning. After that we were dismissed to go back and put on our overalls and get on with our work. When we got back our Commanding Officer was furiously demanding to know where we had been and when we told him he stormed off and that was the last time we had to parade in the morning, nor were we required to do guard duties, much to the disgust of the station staff. The station staff never did get on with the commanding officers, they were always at loggerheads with each other. We did not mind as it made life interesting and we could get on with our work without what we thought unnecessary interruptions.

We would go into Newcastle in the evenings to see if we could get some cigarettes. We would make a round of the pubs, ask for half a pint and then ask if they had any cigarettes. By the time we did get some we could see double.

One day our CO had us on parade and introduced us to our new Warrant Officer who would be in charge of administration. He was taken down the ranks of the men and introduced to each man and we found he remembered each man, and his name after that. As he went down the line he looked at one man a few away from me and said, 'Don't I know you?' and the man said, 'I don't think so, Sir.' Warrant Officer moved off and then came back again and said, 'I do know you. Didn't you try to join up in Glasgow?'

'Yes, sir.' And the Warrant Officer said, 'Do you remember what I told you then?'

'Was I sure that I wanted to join up.'

'Well, you changed your mind.' This Warrant Officer became regarded as a formidable officer with the squadron.

One day we all had to be issued with new identity cards and we had to go to the orderly room to get these cards issued. I went along and found myself in front of this Warrant Officer to have my new card issued. He asked me for my details and rank and so on, and then he asked my age, and my mind went a complete and wonderful blank and I just stared at him. He shouted out, 'Look at this imbecile, he doesn't know how old he is. What year were you born, sonny?' And I couldn't think of that either.

One morning we were called up on parade and taken to the stores where we were issued with tropical kit with khaki shorts and jackets, and also rifles. We wondered what on earth was going to happen. We were sent up to Greenock docks where we boarded a ship which was not actually in the docks but moored out in what was called Greenock Loch. The planes were left behind at Newcastle. When we got on board we found we had proper cabin accommodation, which we thought was lovely. We were drilled as though we were going to invade another country and we had to climb down a rope ladder down the side of the ship with a heavy pack and our rifles. This was very awkward as the weight of the pack would make us swing away from the side of the ship. At the bottom of the rope there were landing craft and they took us over to the shore and we were taken off on route marches. We were counted off in twelves and each twelve had to march in single file each side of the road. We were told that this was to avoid loss of life if we were strafed by aircraft, which would happen if we all marched in a group together.

Sometimes we were taken off by lorry into the countryside and then dropped and had to make our own way back. We had to return to the landing craft which would take us back to the ship. One day I found I had lost my Pay Book which is a very serious offence as if it fell into the wrong hands the information could be used for all sorts of nefarious purposes. So I thought up what I thought was a very convincing explanation. I went to the Sergeant on duty and told him that as I was getting up on to my bunk, which was the top bunk by the port hole, my Pay Book fell out of my top pocket and out of the port hole. Where upon I dashed out onto the deck to try to retrieve it just in time to watch it disappear under the water. To demonstrate its disappearance from sight I made fluttery motions with my hands. The Sergeant looked at me and went, 'Hmm. I am not sure I understand quite what you mean, perhaps you could go through it again, using this desk as an approximation of your bunk.' So I went through it all again with the same fluttery hand movements all the while beginning to feel extremely foolish and hot and sweaty. At the end of this second performance the Sergeant shifted in his seat and then looking me in the eye he asked if I was sure the Pay Book had definitely gone where no one else could get at it, which I assured him was the case.

'Well,' he said, 'just to be sure we have it all correctly would you just go through that one more time.' So I went through the whole performance again with the fluttering hands and all, wishing I was anywhere else but there. Then he stared at me again and eventually said, 'Marsh, when you look at me what do you see?'

'A Sergeant, sir.'

'Well, do I look like a bloody idiot? Even if that story was true it would be difficult enough to believe. Here,' he said, and threw my Pay Book unto the table. 'I found it in the toilet.' Oh dear. Anyway, he was decent enough not to take the matter further.

In order to find something for us to do, the officers got us stripping down the three donkey engines on board. These were small engines which were used to lift stores out of the hold and so on. Then we found there was a store of peanuts on board, and after a while we began to look like peanuts. However we were wondering what was going on as we were not doing anything that we had been trained to do, and after all, there was a war going on. Then one day there was a message over the tannoy that we were all to parade on deck the next morning, when we would be issued with leave passes and we would be going home on leave as soon as the passes were signed. After our leave we were to report back for duty in Elgin in Scotland.

On returning from our leave we were met at Elgin station by lorries who took us off into the countryside and we found ourselves billeted in Nissen huts in the grounds of a large country house. The grounds were large enough to contain a lake of its own which I believe was called St Mary's Loch. We found our kit had been brought over from the ship for us and once we had sorted ourselves out and settled in we were each day loaded into the lorries and taken out over the bonny hills of Scotland and left to find our own way back. Then one day our company were told to get out our tropical jackets, which were khaki, and the two companies were then taken out into the countryside and we had to pretend we were the enemy and we had to hunt out each other. One morning we woke to find the other company had spent the night sleeping under a bridge which we could see below us. We managed to sneak down without being seen, and having loaded our rifles with blanks managed to 'kill' the other company who were very annoyed and accused us of taking an unfair advantage. They appealed to our umpire but he just found it very funny. There was a small pub nearby and in the evening we were told we could go in groups and have a drink. Needless to say we all ended up there and drank the pub dry. The local people had initially found the situation alarming as they thought we were Germans, but when they realised what was going on they were very hospitable and would feed us sandwiches and cake. However, none of us could understand why we were doing this, and to this day I do not know what we were supposed to be doing.

However, what with living out on the hills and the long marches we were very fit. Then we were sent back to Newcastle and our planes sitting on the tarmac. We were there in Newcastle for quite a while, and then we were told we would be sent home on leave and we would be posted abroad on our return.

CHAPTER FOUR

We boarded ship in Liverpool after our leave. We were expecting to have similar accommodation in this ship as we had on board the ship in Greenock Loch, but no such luck. We were all accommodated in one large deck that had mess tables and benches running down the middle, and down the sides, racks of hammocks. Not good.[1]

There were hooks in the ceiling that you were supposed to attach the hammock to. While some of the men seemed to be able to sleep in hammocks I never got the hang of it and slept on the floor. Some men slept on the tables. Not very hygienic. When the ship sailed the sailors came and bolted the portholes shut and then fixed heavy steel shutters over them so that we should not show any light,

---

[1] When Harold was sent off on the naval convoy of course he had no idea where he was going, but that convoy was intended to go to Iraq because of the oilfields there. Then the Iraqi rulers were pro-German, and Prime Minister Winston Churchill was afraid of the German threat to cut off the oil supply from the UK. It has been speculated that the reason the squadron was given such intensive commando-style training before being shipped off was possibly that it was anticipated that the British troops would have to fight themslves ashore to establish airfields, and that they would have to continue fighting to defend them. Their tropical kit would have been equally suitable for Iraq and Singapore.

so we were living down there in artificial light. Some nights if the weather was good we would go and sleep out on deck as it soon became very smelly down below. When we started out we were in convoy and the weather was not good.

I could then appreciate why my father talked me out of joining the Navy. When you are fighting on the land the targets are spread out and the chances are that your assailant will miss you, but on the sea in a ship you are the only target and it was a very uncomfortable feeling. There were enemy submarines around and our convoy consisted of destroyers and some little ships called corvettes. I would have hated to have been on one of those. When the sea was rough you would see them perched up on the top of a wave and the next minute they would disappear as they slipped down into a trough and then back up again. It made me feel sick just looking at them. We had to zigzag and sail in a big arc in order to avoid the enemy submarines. I do not remember how long it took us to cross but eventually we got into warmer climes and the smell below got worse. There seemed to be no air down there.

One meal time we were sitting at the mess tables having our meal when the Medical Officer came down and announced that he would be having an FFI inspection. This means Free From Infection inspection of the unmentionables. The row facing us had to stand on their benches with their trousers down while we were still continuing with our meal. When it came to our turn the row behind us had a view of our bare bottoms. There were a lot wisecracks were flying about and what made it worse was that we were having sausages for our dinner!

One day they had a practice and fired their guns. What a noise.

Our first port of call was Durban on the coast of South Africa which seemed like heaven to us. Of course we had put on our tropical kit by this time and when we were given leave to go into Durban we all felt very uncomfortable as our standard issue of shorts were long and came below the knees. Although that is fashionable now, then we all felt proper 'nanas walking about like that, but it was the same for everyone and we had to put up with it. Some of the lads got invited out for meals but that didn't happen to us so one of the lads said he would soon fix that and at the next crossroads we came to he had us standing pointing in different directions as though we did not know which way to go. A car soon pulled up and asked us where we wanted to go to and we told the driver we were looking to see which direction it was for the quayside. The man told us to get in and he would take us, which he did, but he also took us for a good meal on the way and we thought ourselves very lucky. That leave did not last long and too soon the ship left Durban. We still had no idea where we were going.

We found we were then on a long journey, and the officers tried to keep us active and fit on board and arranged sports for us on deck which we had to take part in. We found it very difficult to run on the pitching deck. They got us playing what we then called Housey Housey and other games to pass the time.

Members of 232 Squadron in Singapore.

Then we arrived in Singapore. The airfield at Singapore was called Seletar. We were marched to our camp and found that our billets were huts made of reeds. They were built on two levels. We slept on the top level and stored our kit on the bottom level. We slept under mosquito nets.

Our planes had come with us on the ship and we had to get them unloaded and reassembled. These were then the most modern planes on that airfield. All the other planes there were just some old biplanes. However, a flyer who had been in the East for some time told us that however impressive we thought the Hurricanes were they were no match for the Japanese fighters which had obviously been built for tropical conditions. The only way for the Hurricanes to have the advantage over the Japanese planes was to try to get above them and then shoot them up as they dived down through them. The Japanese were subjecting the area to what was called pattern bombing. They would pick a target and all the planes would drop all their bombs on that target and if you were in that area you had a rough time. There were slit trenches for us to shelter in at our dispersal point.

Also, around the air field there were monsoon ditches, storm drains, around the camp with large drainage conduits which were like tunnels and passed under the roadway and into what appeared to be a country club of some sort across the road from the airfield. This obviously catered for the smart set as it had tennis courts and a golf course. When we got the planes off we would run across the airfield, through one of these tunnels under the road and across the golf course and get in one of the slit trenches over there as we were then further away from the bombing. One day we watched the old planes, which had a pilot and a co-pilot seated behind, as they took off. They never came back. I don't know if they were all shot down or landed somewhere else.

One day our planes took off, with the exception of the Commanding Officer who for some reason was not flying that day. As soon as the planes took off, so did we. We ran through the storm drains onto the golf course and we were halfway across when there were a couple of shots fired above our heads. We stopped and looked round and saw the CO coming after us in a complete rage. He shouted at us and cursed us saying we were a disgrace and we should take shelter where we were told, calling us yellow-livered so-and-sos. So we all went back to the trenches at the dispersal point. That day, as it happened, we were targeted by the Japanese and they plastered us. I watched as one plane dive-bombed the road where one of the tunnels was underneath with some of our men sheltering in it. The road took a direct hit but fortunately the tunnel and the men survived. They were not badly injured but suffered from blast. As we were attempting to clear up afterwards the CO came and apologised and gave us permission to continue what we had been doing. He told us that he realised that while in the air the flyers could take evasive action, but on the ground you just have to take what is thrown at you. He arranged for the lorry drivers to take us in their trucks into the rubber plantations as soon as the planes were airborne and bring us back when the planes came back.

I never did get into Singapore to have a look around. We were told that we would soon be evacuated as the Japanese were getting closer. The bulk of the stores had already been evacuated. We had, all of us, fancied a pair of flying boots. Don't know why as it is a tropical country. But one night, being very bored, we broke into the stores and helped ourselves to a pair of flying boots. It was only when we got them back to our billets we realised we had all got right boots only. The boots were packed into crates, one crate right boots and the other crate, left.

Then one day we were told that our evacuation was imminent. The Hurricanes were fuelled and armed and made ready to leave. We were the last remaining squadron in the area. We saw the planes off. We were put on lorries and taken to the docks. We lost all our kit. As we went through the town we saw the soldiers there digging trenches. They waved as we went by. I felt terrible. It felt as though they were being deserted. There was nothing we could do about it. We didn't even have a pea shooter between us.

We landed next in Sumatra which was a Dutch colony. As I remember it was not a very long journey. We were divided into two groups, one lot was to look after the planes and the other lot had to get the billets organised and get some kit together. We heard that Singapore had fallen shortly after we had passed through.

It didn't take long to get ourselves sorted out as we were only in a field. Again as soon as our planes had taken off we would dash into the jungle. This was where I discovered pineapples. The natives would cut them so they were in a sort of spiral still attached to the stalk, and oh they were delicious. One day when we ran into the jungle I leaned against a tree which unfortunately had a red ants nest at the base. In seconds I was smothered in little red ants and oh how they bit me. I had to strip off while my mates shook what they could out of my clothes. It was very embarrassing and very painful. I cannot remember how long we were there but it wasn't very long.

One evening I had a message that I had to report to the Provost Marshal, who was the officer in charge of the Service Police. When I reported at the station headquarters I was shown in to a Sergeant SP and it was explained why I was there. Two airmen had gone out to a shop one evening to buy something and had signed for their purchases. However, one had paid and the other one had not and one had very kindly signed my name. I was fortunate in that the one who had paid was the one that had signed my name. I was told I would be in just as much trouble if I didn't tell them who the other one was, which I couldn't as I didn't know anything about it. After the interview was over I was told to go and sit in the next room. I had been sitting there for about half an hour when a general panic seemed to break out. Men were rushing in and out of offices and then some men came rushing out carrying bundles of paper and started a bonfire with them in the square outside. When I asked what was going on I was told that the Japanese had invaded Sumatra, at the bottom end of the island, and were advancing on us. I didn't want to be captured with a load of people who were complete strangers so I took a chance and got up and started to leave the building. A Sergeant shouted at me asking what I thought I was doing and I said I was going to return to my squadron. 'No you won't,' he shouted, 'there will be a lorry along here in a minute with ammunition and rifles and you are to get yourself a rifle and wait here.' Which is what I did and then I sat and waited again. Then an officer appeared who asked me what I was doing there as he realised I was not station headquarters staff. I told him what I had been told to do and he told me to hand back the rifle and to try to return to my squadron. I went off down the road. It was about half an hour's walk from the town and as I approached the town I saw three or four of my mates walking along the road and I joined them and asked what they were doing. I was told that they had orders to get to the docks and get over to the other side of the river.

As we were running we could see great clouds of black smoke over the other side of the river. We got to the river only to see that the ferry had just left. We could see that the oilfields were being set alight by the British to prevent them

Oilfields being set on fire in Sumatra by British troops.

falling into Japanese hands. And then there was an air raid. Some of my mates had managed to get aboard the ferry but they all started to jump off and struggle to the bank as they did not want to be on the ferry if it got strafed. We went along the river bank and managed to find a native who would take us across in his canoe for payment. The river was very fast flowing and we were taken quite a way down the river by the current. It was very hair-raising with the air raid going on at the same time but we thought we would be safer crossing this way. Once again we had lost all our kit.

We made our way back up to where the ferry would have docked and we found there was a Sergeant of the Service Police who was directing people and he told us that our squadron was to go on to the next airfield. We set off. After about 5 or 6 miles we saw one of our Hurricanes down in a swamp at the side of the road. A couple of us got a native to paddle us over to it in a canoe and we had a look inside. There were bullet holes in the cockpit and blood on the wing where the pilot had obviously got out but we never did find out what happened to him. The parachute was missing from the cockpit. We had no way of telling if he had used it or if it had been stolen after the plane landed. For all we know the pilot may have fallen into the swamp and drowned. We continued on down the road. Lorries kept passing us, going down to the ferry landing stage and picking up people. If they had any room on their return they would pick up some of the people walking along the road. We walked quite a long way but eventually we were picked up by a lorry driver and taken the rest of the way to the airfield where we would be working.

After we had been there a while working on the planes half of us were told to go to the native village nearby to see if we could get some food, which we were unable to do. On the way back to base we saw the other half of the armourers walking towards us and they told us they had been told to make their way to the rail head a couple of miles or so away. Our lot had drawn the short straw and were to prepare the planes for one last sortie before we also left. Just our luck. The remainder of the Hurricanes took off and we had to wait until they landed. The pilots had been instructed that on their return to base they were to land with the wheels up in order to make them unusable to the enemy. We had to stand by in case any of the pilots needed assistance. Of course, landing with the wheels up rendered the planes unfit

Group photograph taken in Singapore. Those men marked with a cross were reported missing and not heard of again.

for any future use as the undercarriage and propellers were completely wrecked.

Then we started another long walk, this time to the railway station. We met up with the rest of our mates but there was a problem. The local railway drivers refused to drive the engine. Strangely enough, and I never did find out what they were doing there, but there were two men from the Navy and one was a stoker and he volunteered to have a go at driving the engine. The train consisted of the engine, of course, and several box cars. We slid the doors of one of the box cars open and we all got in. The train started off OK and we sat on the floor of the box car dangling our legs over the side and enjoyed the fresh air, just hoping the Navy stoker would know how to stop the blinking thing. Men were breaking up parts of the box cars to fuel the engine's furnace That was all OK until someone decided they wanted to go to the toilet so we just slid the box car doors almost closed and several of us passed water out through the narrow gap. That was OK until someone decided they wanted to do something more serious and we told him that no way was he going to do that in the box car; we did not know how long we were going to be there and for all we knew we might have to pass the night there. So we slid the doors until there was a gap of about a couple of foot and we dangled him outside. Just to be on the safe side, two men held on to his feet and two held on to his hands. That must have been the most uncomfortable toilet he had ever done before or since.

Eventually we arrived at the docks. We were told to get off and parade and a roll call was taken and a few of the lads were missing and we never did know what happened to them. Eventually we were marched onto a small, ancient Dutch cargo boat. We were put down in the hold, not very First Class, but we weren't bothered as long as we were going to get away. The Warrant Officer in charge of us, whom I described previously, was still with us and he was offered one of the few cabins there were but he refused saying that if his men were down below then that was good enough for him. We all admired him for that. There were not very many crew left to handle the ship so we were ordered to help out. Our cooks went down into the galley but it was soon discovered there was really not enough food on board to feed all of us, and not enough plates and cups and so on. The ship was packed out with over 2,000 men on board, for which it was not equipped. We just had to make the best of it and find what space we could. At night we could hear rats running about.[2]

The engineers went to help out in the engine room in the charge of the ship's engineer, and we armourers we were told that we had to look after a small gun that was on deck at the stern, under the command of one of the ship's crew. We went off to have a look at it and decided that we would sink the Japanese Navy if it happened to pass by. The crew member got us practising with some dummy shells which were made of wood and we got one of these shells stuck in the gun barrel. We were in full view of the officers in the bridge so we all huddled round the gun so they could not see what we were up to, and got a broom handle and hammered that down the barrel until we got it out.

We had no idea where we were being taken to but eventually we arrived in Columbo in Ceylon, which is now called Sri Lanka. When we arrived we found out that the Japanese had taken the port in Sumatra the morning after we had left. We had left after dark the evening before and we found out that we must have sailed through the Japanese

---

[2]   The ship was Dutch and was called the *Kota Gede*; the captain was Frederick Goos, the crew a mixed one of Dutch and Indonesians. Apparently his instructions were to sail to Australia, but he sailed to Ceylon, which probably saved the lives of the people on board as most of the shipping to Australia was sunk by the Japanese. The captain expected to be court-martialled for this, but as he saved the lives of about 2,000 servicemen, this could hardly be done.

invasion force. We were very lucky that we had got away. Maybe we owed our survival to the Japanese not wanting to blow an old cargo boat out of the water and give the game away to the people on the shore. Also I realised that I had had my twenty-first birthday while crossing the Indian Ocean. I had spent my birthday sitting on that little pea shooter on the back of that little ship. Never mind.

Harold and his 'peashooter' on the Kota Gede *and other members of gun crew. Harold on the right at front.*

Chapter Five

We were put on another ship and then we sailed off again up the west coast of India and arrived in Karachi in what is now Pakistan. It was a regular peace-time camp. We were housed in tents and the camp got larger and larger as we were joined by others who had managed to get away from the Japanese. The camp was on the edge of a desert which meant that you were eating sand and drinking sand and it wasn't very nice at all. It was very, very hot and there were flies everywhere and very soon nearly everyone had dysentery. We would report sick and would be given a large dose of caster oil and told not to eat for two or three days. That usually did the trick, and by that time we would all be ravenously hungry and go down to the NAAFI and have a good stoke up with food.

We were given mosquito nets. Sheets were a luxury and you were very seldom issued with sheets. I think that of the seven years I served in the RAF for five of those years I was not given sheets. I just slept with blankets. We were issued with new kit, including new shorts, which were not short at all, but long. They were very uncomfortable to wear and we hated them.

There was nothing to do in the camp. We were waiting

On the move in India.

for someone to decide what to do with us. Boredom set in and quite a few of the lads got up to mischief to pass the time. The camp was on a camel route and quite often native traders would pass by, sitting on camels fast asleep. Some of the lads would creep out and turn the camels round so they would walk off back the way they came.

Eventually the day came when somebody decided what to do with us and we were sent to Peshawar on the North-West Frontier near the Khyber Pass. This is where a lot of the trouble is nowadays. Even then we were not allowed to go into Peshawar as we were told that all the tribesmen carried arms and knives and rifles, and it was said to be too dangerous for us to go there. We were re-equipped and given some planes to service. They were American planes called Mohawks and we all thought they were horrible. Two of the guns fired through the propellers and if you did not get the timing right the propellers would be shot off. We would go down to the firing range and the planes would come over for practice.[3]

There was a concrete bunker for us to shelter in where we would be taken under guard. We would run up a red flag at the commencement of firing and we were locked in. We were told that the bunker was to preserve us from the natives in the hills as much as anything else. As soon as we ran the red flag down at the end of firing practice the hills around would come alive with tribesmen who would rush down and dig up the spent bullets, and they would make all their own ammunition and even their own rifles, so I was told.

There was a fort up in the Khyber Pass which was held by the British and we had to go there sometimes to practise. There was a small aeroplane with the garrison and if the tribesmen fired on the fort with their cannon the plane would be sent over to bomb the villages as reprisal. They would first warn that the bombing would take place so that the civilians in the villages could take to the hills. The villages would be searched for the cannon but they were never found as they would be dismantled and hidden in caves. If you were stationed in the fort you had a pretty miserable time as you were not allowed to smoke in the open after dark or wear white, as a sniper would have a go at you. I was due to

---

[3] When Harold arrived in Karachi he was posted to Peshawar, which was and still is a very dangerous place to be. The mountain tribes in the Khyber Pass area had always traditionally fought each other, and when the British became the nominal rulers the native tribesmen took on the British as well. You get a glimpse of this in Harold's narrative when they took their bearer with them to the hill station and then had to send him back as the local tribes who were hillmen would not accept him as he was a plainsman.

go with a convoy up to the fort at one time to help take up supplies, but then it was cancelled and I was disappointed as I would have liked to have seen it even though it was very dangerous there. Nobody ever went there in a lorry alone and everyone was issued with a rifle and ammunition and all travel was in a convoy accompanied by armoured cars. Inside the fort were old Army billets where there were iron racks bolted to the floor and the rifles were bolted into the iron racks with thick chains. Even so, as the story went, when the men woke in the morning they found the chains sawn through and the rifles gone.

However, after the sun and sand and the arid conditions in Karachi, it was beautiful and green around Peshawar and I began to feel that I was living like a lord. I had been given my Corporal stripes by then. We had what was called a bearer. This was a job which was handed down from father to son and had probably been so for centuries. This was an Army custom that had been in place ever since the British Army had been in India. Our bearer did everything for us, we did not have to do anything for ourselves. There would be eight or nine men to a hut and as I was now Corporal I was charged with looking after them. We used to pay the bearer, each of us, 1 rupee a week, which in English money was about one and sixpence. I gave the bearer his money at the end of the first week and the boy who did all the work came to me and told me that the bearer only gave him a rupee for what he did, and he did all the work, and out of that 1 rupee he had to buy the polish and anything else that was needed. So at the end of the second week I gave the boy all the money except for 1 rupee which I gave to the bearer. The bearer became very angry and agitated and shouted at us that he would take the matter to the CO. We said he could do that if he wanted, we didn't mind. He told us that he had credentials, and he dashed off and brought us in this letter. I really cannot repeat here what was written on that bit of paper, In effect the 'credentials' said that if this so-and-so gentleman came within kicking distance then we were to kick his ---- as far as we could. Unfortunately for him, although he could speak English he could not read it. Anyway, he left and the boy stayed with us. He did everything for us, all we had to do was dress and undress. He would even shave us, even if we were asleep. If we had a kit inspection he would lay out our kit for us, and better than we would do it. When we had an early morning shift he would wake us up with a cup of tea, and when we went out in the evening he would lay out all our clean clothes. He would polish our shoes until you could see your face in them but then as you were leaving the hut he would rush up with a duster and give the shoes an extra dust off. There was a man called a 'char-wallah' who would walk around the camp with a tea-urn and you could have a mug of tea any time. Our bearer took away our dirty washing and it would come back clean and beautifully pressed even to crisp creases down the shorts. To us it all seemed like a life of luxury.

One bad thing, though, was that at intervals we would all get something called 'dhobi rash'. *Dhobi* is the Hindi word for washing, laundry, and this would be a red, raw rash around the unmentionables, caused by heat and sweat. We reported sick. We were told to go into a hut at the back of

Harold on leave in the hill country.

the medical office where we would find bottles of stuff we were told to dab on the affected parts with the cotton wool provided. Which we did, and then we found out why the hut had Entry and Exit doors, as after you dabbed the stuff on you fled the hut in agony. Anyone coming in would have got killed by us rushing back to our billet and dashing under the showers, which were cold water only, to try to wash the stuff off. After we had been there a while it was decided that in order for us to recuperate we would be sent to a hill station, called Murree, in the hills just to the north of Rawalpindi, built by the British for the use of their garrison troops in Rawalpindi.

Our bearer wanted to stay with us so he paid for his ticket to come with us on the train but unfortunately when we got there he was not allowed to stay with us as he was considered to be a plainsman, whereas all the bearers there were hill tribes, so we had another bearer and he was nowhere near as good as our own bearer. Our own bearer would wash all our crockery and cutlery for us and lay it all out neatly on our lockers but this bearer would wash everything up and tip it all in a heap in the middle of the table. Nobody could tell whose mug and cutlery etcetera belonged to who. We had a Scotsman in the group and he got fed up with this so he tied a piece of string round his mug handle and around the handles of his cutlery and indicated to the bearer that these were his property. When we came in the next time we found the bearer had tied string round the handles of everything and still left it all in a heap in the middle of the table. I won't say what the Scotsman called him but it was rather rude. It was lovely and cool up at the hill station and I suppose we were there for about two weeks and then we were on the train back to Peshawar.

Being on a train in India was nothing like being on a train back home. For one thing, the journeys were much longer and it was nothing to spend two days on the journey. The carriages were not upholstered, just wooden seats, and the toilets were just a hole in the floor with a handle to hang on to. The Indians used to cling on all over the train, with some sitting on the roof, so that it didn't look like a train at all, just a mass of people hanging on the move. There were stories of people falling off and being killed or being dragged off by the draught when another train passed by. After our life of comparable luxury in Murree we found our way back to our airstrip; which was just that. Just a strip of grass and the huts with not even a village nearby. We settled down to our usual routine and I think we were there for quite some time Then we found we were to have another train journey as we were to be posted to Madras.

Madras is a large city on the south-east coast of India. There wasn't a lot for us to do there when off duty. No cinemas. We would go out to try and find cafes where we could go. We used to get up teams playing football among the different sections. Our canteen and cookhouse there were two separate buildings, one about 10 yards from the other. There were birds that used to perch on the roof of the cookhouse, some sort of hawk I think, and as we emerged with our plates of food from the cookhouse the birds would swoop down and steal your dinner. We swore that they must have been fitted with vacuum cleaners as even if you had stew that would somehow disappear. We had to resort to putting our hats over our plate; we would be caught only a couple of times. But it was funny to see new people arriving and unexpectedly losing their dinner.

We were just leading ordinary ordinary, boring lives there, the same routine every day. When we went down to the town we would take a rickshaw back, which was just a seat on wheels pulled by an Indian in the shafts. By this time we had got rid of all our old service issue uniforms. We got our uniforms made up for us by local tailors. It was all khaki just the same but our shorts were shorter and neater and the shirts were better and well fitting. We had smarter tunics made to our measurements and better topees than the ones

Harold under canvas in Madras. Harold on the left with 2 friends,
Bill and Paddy.

we had been issued with. We were all dressed up to the nines.
Down in the town we would find bars where we could go
in for a drink. I suppose we managed to amuse ourselves
somehow or another. Eventually this all came to an end,
again, and we were moved on to a place called Visakhapatam
where we were under canvas.

I would lie in bed at night listening to the hyenas making
a noise. I wasn't bothered then as I just thought they were
some sort of dog but now I understand they can be quite
ferocious. We could see the hyenas wandering around
between the tents making their horrible noise, but like
everything else we got used to it. We had to empty our shoes
in the morning in case there were scorpions in them. And
we had to check our bedclothes before getting into them in
case of snakes. I suppose I was very lucky during my service
career as I generally kept very well. Apart from the dhobi

Brew up on the road.

rash and dysentery I never had much go wrong with me apart from prickly heat, which is a rather horrible itchy rash. Quite a lot of the lads got malaria which was not very nice.

We had every third day off so that you could do your laundry and other chores. We had nothing to do once we had tended to our planes. We did not dare touch them again after we had serviced them in case an emergency came up. We coped with the boredom as best we could. Then we found we were on the move again and were taken to the nearest railway stop for another long journey across the Indian countryside. After quite a long while the train started to rock about in a violent manner and came to a stop. We did not know what on earth was happening but afterwards we were told we had been on the edge of a hurricane? What we had experienced was bad enough, what must it have been like in the centre of the hurricane. We waited a long while for the wind to drop and eventually the train started again.

We got further along the railway line and the train stopped again at an Indian village. We were told that a brick bridge further along the line had blown down. Of course the village had suffered badly in the hurricane. Quite a few people had been killed, as well as cattle. We got off the train to have a look around. Near the railway tracks there was a small brick building and we could see that there was an elderly woman just lying inside. Our MO went over and tended her as best he could but she died. We could not believe what we saw next, as two men came up and tied her wrists and ankles together, slung her on a pole and took her over to the paddy fields where they just dumped her, and the vultures came down and ate her. There were quite a few dead cattle lying around and, I suppose with the heat, they had swollen up like balloons, but people were just walking about taking no notice.

We lived for a couple of days on bully-beef and hard tack. There seemed to be plenty of tea so being British we were OK. Then we boarded the train again and travelled to where the bridge was down, unloaded our supplies from the train, manhandled it all across the ravine and got on another train which took us to Calcutta. It had in all taken us about a week to get to Calcutta. In Calcutta we were billeted at the race course and we were housed in what had been the stands when they had had the races before the war. It was a well-known race course before the war.

Calcutta was quite a nice place, certainly after some of the places we had stayed in, out in the wilds. We were alongside a main road where trams ran and on the other side there was a park, and some shops, cinemas and Chinese restaurants. The main place there I believe was called Dalboys where quite a lot of the men went for a meal and you could get a drink there. The Chinese restaurants were very popular and the food there was very good, not like the Chinese restaurants at home. It was nice being back in civilisation and being able to go out for a meal and have a drink and to go to the cinema, like normal. I went out one night on my own and being young and foolish I ended up having a tattoo on my arm. The Chinese Quarter was out of bounds, but one night the lads and I decided we would have a look around and of course we got caught by the Service Police. We pleaded we did not know as we had just got back from the Far East, and they let us off with a caution.

We became very friendly with an Indian who owned a restaurant. His wife was English. He invited us to his house one evening and we were bowled over by the photographs that he had taken. He had a real genius for photography. He would not just go and take a snapshot as we would do. If he wanted a view of a particular place he would visit that place several times and spend a lot of time deciding where and at what angle he would take that particular shot.

Back in the stands at the race course we were pretty comfortable. We had string beds which we would cover with a mat and a blanket. At night sitting in your bed surrounded by the mosquito net it was like being in a little tent of your own. We were there for about two months, when we were told we would be on the move again. We were taken to the railway station and put on the train again. We were on the train for a long time. Eventually the train stopped at a landing place on a very big river where we were loaded onto quite a large ship, a ferry I suppose, and we loaded all our stuff and kit, and were taken up river. We had been on the boat for quite a few hours when it stopped and we had to unload all our stuff and kit and get onto another train.

We eventually stopped at a place called Dimapur where we spent the night. Dimapur was a transit camp and near the Burma border. The next morning we were put on lorries with our supplies and kit and we were told we were going to a place called Imphal. This was a journey of about eight days or more. The lorries had mostly English drivers and a few Indians. We were told that the Indians were taught to drive, then given a truck and sent off, and if they arrived at their destination over the mountains they were judged to have passed their driving test. Presumably the ones who did not arrive at the destination were judged to have failed. The journey seemed to go on forever with lots of hold-ups due to landslides or lorries going over the edge, and some days we were on the lorries for 12 hours or more. We went through Kohima and on the way we passed the District Commissioner's house which was a huge colonial mansion with tennis courts. It was a beautiful spot, surrounded by huge trees.

When we arrived at our camp we were tired and feeling very dusty and dirty and asked where we could have a shower. We were told the only place was the river, which was just a short distance from the camp. So we went there and the river looked lovely although it was quite fast flowing. It looked so inviting so we undressed and jumped in. I lost my breath as the water was so cold. Of course the river came down off the mountains. However we stuck it out and we got to like it as it was so refreshing. Our camp was basic, the huts were built of reeds. It got very cold at night. We dug a hole in the floor at the end of our hut so we could have a fire. We would throw bits of bamboo poles in it to burn.

The first day we were there our Flight Sergeant thought up the idea of making a gun pit with a couple of spare guns on tripods. We thought he was a bit scatty but we followed him through some long grass to a higher piece of ground, and as we emerged from the grass we had a fit as we were all covered in leeches. We did not realise this until we could actually see them. Some were quite big where they had already sucked our blood. Some of the lads went nuts and tried pulling them off and someone shouted at them to stop it as if you do that they leave their heads under the skin. We lit cigarettes and touched them with the lighted end and they would drop off. Like everything else, we got used to it. We never did use the gun pit.

Apparently the Japanese were only a few miles from us. We had patrols out everywhere. Our aircraft were told not to bomb anything within 20 miles of our camp. The Mohawks, the American planes we had, could carry about ten small bombs on board, anti-personnel bombs, as well as their other armament and they would go off every day strafing and bombing. The only trouble was, as soon as Japanese troop movement was seen, say on a hill, and the information radioed back to the camp, the hill would have been taken by our own side and the aeroplanes would bomb our own men.

After about a week we were moved from our reed huts to some larger huts that appeared to be made out of mud and cow dung with a thatched roof. Surprisingly, they were quite nice and quite substantial. There was a verandah in the front and a smooth patio made of mud where we would play Pitch and Toss for money. We had been there a few days and a little girl came round, called Mimo. She was carrying her little baby brother and another brother, a toddler, walked behind her. We were amused that the only piece of clothing the toddler wore was a piece of string tied round his tummy with his John Thomas hanging out, so we cut out a little piece of material and hung it from the string in the front but he just screamed until we took it off. These children came round every day. The people up there were among the nicest we had come across and were very pleasant and would wave as we walked by. We came to know that the hut we were living in had been Mimo's family house; we did not know how it had come that we were billeted there, whether they had been paid or whatever, but as I say the people there were very friendly. They were never on the scrounge, just the opposite: they would bring us fruit and other odds and ends. The children would play on the verandah and were very well behaved and would never enter the hut.

Our only washing facilities was still the river. The natives would come and do their washing in the river and wash their pots and pans so it was not what you would call hygienic. But we would go and have a swim every day – well, sort of swim, as I still cannot swim to this day – but it was refreshing. In the end of our hut there was a fairly deep hole with a little bit of water in the bottom, only about 6 inches deep, I suppose, and one day the little lad fell in it. I fished him out, hardly got my feet wet, but the next day his father came round and treated me as though I was the local hero. I was the cat's whiskers.

The children came round and taught us a song in the local language. One day we were out on the verandah singing this song when a group of young Indian ladies came by and they roared with laughter. Whether the children had taught us a dirty song as a joke or whether it was our singing we never did know, but the young ladies thought it very funny.

One evening the children came round and took our hands and dragged us off. We did not know where we were going but we came into the village where an area was decorated with fairy lights, not electric lights but paraffin lamps with coloured glass in front of them. They were having a concert of some sort. All the women were all dressed up in fantastically beautiful coloured dresses, like butterflies. We were pulled to the front and given seats of honour, well, not seats, but on the ground in the front so that we could see the dancing. We did not know what it was all about but it was very interesting and it was nice to have had the experience. We also watched a funeral which was a cremation on a funeral pyre. We watched these things as it was all very interesting.

One of the lads got himself a monkey but the blinking thing was quite mad. I don't know where he got it from, probably bought it from somebody. When we set off in the morning in our trucks we would have to put our tin hats on as the monkey would run across the top of the lorry and try to scratch your head. It would stuff its fist into its mouth and appear to shriek with rage. In the armoury we would have boxes which had held ammunition and they were about 1 foot 6 long, about 10 inches wide and 1 foot deep. We would stack all these boxes on top of each other and this blasted monkey would jump up on the top of them and start them rocking and just as they all fell down he would jump off. The number of times we swore about this monkey.

As I say, the people were very friendly and hospitable, amazing really, as we were living in their homes. I quite enjoyed the time we were there, in spite of a war going on. We had something to do; the planes had to be attended to and we had other things which kept us occupied. The climate was very pleasant, not overbearingly hot as it is in the main part of India, and the nights were cool so we weren't plagued by mosquitoes. The village of Imphal itself was made mostly of mud huts mostly like our billet, and … it did have a cinema! I don't know if it had always been there or if it had been put in for the troops. It wasn't very comfortable. The seats were just forms made up from bamboo poles. It was just down the road from us and we did go once but it was too uncomfortable.

One day while we were working, Orde Wingate's troops went by. These were troops specially trained in jungle warfare. It was said they could live on a tin of bully beef and a packet of biscuits if they had to. I noticed that some of the men were Air Force wireless operators. They all went off up into the jungle. The air strip where we were ran parallel to the road and we watched them as they all marched along the road with their mules. They carried all their equipment, everything they wanted, with them.

Chapter Six

We had a chance to go on leave from there and we thought 'Why not' and about a dozen of us went. We were taken by truck to the railway which took us back to the ferry. It was a long trip on the ferry and a few of the men started playing cards for money and by the time the ferry docked they had lost all their money so they stayed on the boat and went straight back. You could never tell some of these half-daft lot anything. We went down to Calcutta, it took us about two days. At the railway station there were Service Police at the barrier so that nobody could get away with anything. We had to go to the Rail Transport Officer and have our leave passes stamped and our two weeks holiday started from then. We had quite a good time there. We went to the cinema, it was a good cinema with several changes of film, we stuffed ourselves silly with food and at the end of the evening we went to this place where everyone went for a drink. We stayed at the YMCA. I found the Indian with the English wife who had befriended us when we were there previously and we had a couple of meals with them.

Our leave finished and on the road back to Imphal everything came to a halt as a lorry had gone over the edge. It was a lorry with about six men in it with an Indian driver. I was one of those volunteered to go down on ropes to see if there were any survivors, and to our surprise none had been killed but they were well spread out with the impact of the fall. The track across the mountains there was a dreadful bleak and arid place with not a leaf of anything to be seen. We got back to Imphal, and we were not there long before we were told we were going back to Calcutta and we were going to be re-equipped with Spitfires. We were pleased to see the back of the American planes; we didn't like them very much.

This time in Calcutta we were billeted in large houses where the well-to-do had lived, I suppose. I was a Corporal then of course. So when the Orderly Officer made his rounds I would have to accompany him as Orderly Corporal.

Then half the squadron had to take their Spitfires to an airfield a short way away to practice firing their guns and I was lucky enough to be one of those left behind. I was the only one left in one of the big houses and I found a room which I suppose had once been the pantry and I moved my bed in there, found myself a bedside locker and put my clothes and other gear in the cupboards. I was well away, it was all very cosy and I could lock the door.

One day at work one of the Spitfire pilots came to me and said that the panel on the top of one of the wings had come off and been lost while in flight. Of course, at the end of our inspection of the planes we had to sign that everything was in order and to have this happen was a very serious offence. This could have caused the plane to crash. The pilot was very good about it and he jumped into a jeep to where a Spitfire had crashed at the end of the runway and we got a panel off that and fitted it onto his plane. He was very good about it and never told anybody else. I got to know him quite well as he preferred spending time with the lads than going to the officers' mess. He couldn't do that too often as it was not done in those days. He came up to me one day and said that he had been orderly officer the previous day and he said he could not find my billet. I laughed and said that it was a secret. He said he would find it. I had been out one evening and I had been back only a short time when there was a knock on the door and he stood there with some bottles in his hand. I woke up in the morning sitting up in bed leaning against the wall and he was fast asleep in the chair.

Letters home had to be censored and the Duty Officer had to read them and cut out anything that might be sensitive material, but this pilot officer would not read mine or the other lads', which we appreciated, and made sure we did not put anything in them we shouldn't have done.

All good things come to an end and after our training we were told we were to join the rest of the squadron so our life of luxury was over. The camp was about 7 or 8 miles outside Calcutta. The Spitfires would be standing waiting for flying and the engineer would start the engine and it would be left running to 'warm up'. One day one of the Spitfires started off up the runway and taxied up to where the planes would take off. Then one of our pilots came running up saying someone had stolen his plane. The Spitfire revved up and went roaring down the runway to take off, and all hell was loose on the ground and the air gunners were told to shoot it down if it took off. Anyway, whoever it was chickened out at the last minute and stopped. The Air Police rushed over and found that it was one of the Indian Air Force men sitting there, in full kit and flying helmet. Of course he was arrested and marched off. We never did know what happened to him.

It was here that I was playing football in long grass in a pair of Army boots I had scrounged from somewhere. I don't know where we scrounged all the bits and pieces we had. The boots were quite heavy and then I kicked what I thought was the football but it wasn't it was something solid lying in the long grass. Funnily enough it did not hurt, just felt rather strange. I sat down and took my boot off and found that my big toe was at right angles sticking into my other toes. I was put in a lorry and was taken back to the barracks and to the MO. Much to my disgust he tried pulling it out straight. The pain was terrible. After a while he gave up and I was sent to the Service Hospital in Calcutta. The hospital had proper nursing staff, sisters and qualified nurses and the Medical Officers were Squadron Leaders and so on. Anyway I was taken down to theatre late at night and my foot was placed in splints. The amazing thing was that it still did not hurt. I was put in a bed and the nursing sister came and woke me up to give me a sleeping pill. I had the time of my life there. I was there for about four or five days and then I was sent to a convalescent home in Calcutta. I was given a white suit to show that I was in the Air Force but non-combatant. I decided to go out the next morning and then I got a terrible pain in my stomach, I could hardly move. I got on a rickshaw to go back to the convalescent home but I was in so much pain I had to get off that and made my way back as best I could. I reported in to the medical orderly there and he put me in an ambulance and I was sent straight back to the hospital. I was on the operating table that night with acute appendicitis. When I had been in the hospital before with my foot in a splint I would help the nurses hand out the pills and take the mickey out of the ones who had to take horrible pills and medicines, but now here I was having to take them myself and having to put up with the insults of the others. I was in hospital two weeks then, not like today.

At this time I was writing to a young lady, which turned out to be one of the most important things of my life. She had become friends with my aunt Gladys when they were nurses together and I found out that while I was away Gladys had taken her to see my mother in Whitstable where she had learnt all sorts of secrets about me.

We were all sent back to Imphal. When we got to Kohima, I had the shock of my life, as none of the beautiful tall trees around the regional governor's residence were left standing, just blackened stumps about 3 or 4 foot high. While we had been in Calcutta there had been a terrible battle which had been a turning point in the fight between the British and Japanese. At one point the opposing forces were fighting each other for two or three weeks across the tennis courts. There were hundreds killed and I believe that now there is a big monument there commemorating the battle.[4]

---

[4]   At Kohima there is a memorial to the men who died there. The inscription on the monument reads:

> *When you go home*
> *Tell them of us and say*
> *For your tomorrows*
> *We gave our today.*

CHAPTER SEVEN

I was back at Imphal a short while when I was told to report to the Adjutant. He informed me that I was going to be posted home. My father had been trying through the British Legion to get me sent home as my mother was seriously ill and had been asking for me. I was upset to hear my mother was so ill but I was also upset to leave the lads that I had shared so much with over the last few years. So I left Kohima and was sent first of all to a different airfield in Calcutta to the one where I had been previously. It looked very strange to me as the planes there were bombers and I had always looked after fighter aircraft. I was asked what I knew about bombs and I said nothing, and they said 'How come, as you are an Armourer General and you would have been taught about bombs?' so I told them that for the last few years I had never had anything to do with them. They then asked if I could drive a tractor and when I said I couldn't they told me it was my time to learn. They brought out this huge tractor and pushed me onto it, taught me how to stop and start the thing, drove around a few of the roads in the camp and said I could make myself useful with that until I got sent home.

There were no roads as such, just tracks, and as I drove around for practice there was no other traffic except the occasional bullock cart and even I could manage to miss those. I got friendly with another tractor driver and he showed me what to do. The tractors pulled the bomb trolleys up to the planes for loading. We would go down to the railway sidings and pick up the Indian workers for the morning. We would load up and go to the bomb dump and unload, and then by the time we drove to the billets it was dinner time. Then we made another trip in the afternoon and by the time we finished that it was knocking-off time. It was quite a novelty to me, another interesting experience.

I was not long there and I was posted to the transit camp at Bombay. I was there on parade and the names of those to be sent home were read out. My name was one of the last to be called and I was in a sweat in case I was not going. I was told to pack my kit as I was leaving by ship the next day. I had accumulated quite a lot of kit as you carry everything around including blankets. It was no bother as there were plenty of Indians around who would carry it for you for a couple of rupees. I knew I would miss this back home. We boarded ship, same old mess decks. Again the port holes were shut when at sea and of course below decks began to be a bit smelly. They gave everyone a job to do to keep them occupied and of all things I became a Service Policeman. At least I could patrol the decks in the fresh air.

As conditions with the war at sea had improved since we went out, we did not go all round the Cape but came back the shorter way through the Suez Canal. Through the Canal we were allowed to open the port holes and it was strange because although we were on board a troop ship we would see a camel walk by. We were still in convoy but the chances of being torpedoed or bombed were much less than on our outward journey. We landed in Liverpool and were sent to a transit camp. There were a couple of others who had been sent home for the same reason as myself and we had to sort out what we wanted from our kit and take the rest to the stores and then go to the orderly room for a travel warrant and leave passes, and we were then able to go straight home. The other troops would have stayed in the transit camp and then been posted to other stations.

I caught the train to London and by then had missed the last train to Whitstable so I got on the Underground to Burnt Oak which is where my Aunt Gladys was staying doing her nursing training with Una, the young lady that I had been writing to. I did not realise that Burnt Oak was so far out of the centre of London and it took ages to get there and it was pitch black when I arrived and I had no idea where they were living. I found the hospital and went to the gatehouse or lodge of the hospital and asked them if they knew where Greencourt Avenue was, but they didn't. I roamed round and round but I could not find it. A big Alsation dog jumped up at a gate and frightened the life out of me. I saw a window that had a chink of light showing behind the blackout curtain and I knocked at the door there and a man came. I asked him if he knew where Greencourt Avenue was and he said, 'No mate, never heard of it,' and shut the door. I found out later that his house faced directly up Greencourt Avenue. I eventually found it and the time must have been past midnight then. A man came to the door, a Mr Preston, and he guessed who I was and more or less

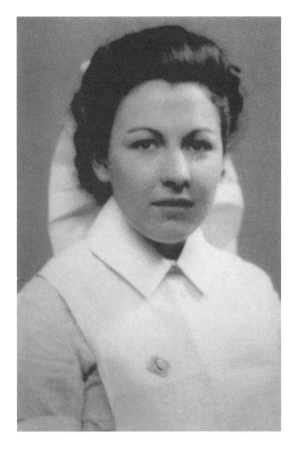

Una Stewart, the future Mrs Harold Marsh

dragged me inside and called down Gladys and Una from upstairs. Some nurses were boarded out from the hospital in case the hospital was hit, as of course in those days most nurses lived in the hospitals.

Poor Gladys had the unpleasant task of having to tell me that I was too late home to see my mother as she had died about two weeks previously. A sad homecoming. And as for the young lady I had been writing to, she was caught how she did not want to be caught, I guess, in her nightgown and curlers. Mr Preston was very good. He made me a meal and a cup of tea and I slept in his bed while he slept in what they called a table shelter. I caught an early train down to Granny Bootes in Faversham. We had a few tears there. My mother had been my grandmother's much-loved eldest daughter. Later, I caught the bus to Whitstable, my home town to see my father. Of course he was out to work all day so he suggested that I spend some time staying with my grandmother. My leave was up Christmas Eve. No way was I going back Christmas Eve having been away all those years, even though Christmas was not very bright under the circumstances, so I went back the day after Boxing Day.

I was to report back to one of the London air bases. I could see two Service Policemen heading for me and I thought I was going to be in some trouble. One of them looked at my leave pass and told me the obvious, that I was overdue, but I explained the circumstances and they sent me on my way telling me to say that I hadn't seen them. The Marsh luck again. I was then sent up to Liverpool and reported to the orderly room and the Duty Sergeant said the same as the Service Police. He then told me my posting had come through and I was going to RAF Colerne near Bath, and gave me my travel warrant. So I picked up some more kit, travelled down to London and then to Croydon and out to Colerne where I found I was to have another cushy job. This squadron had the first jet planes and the base was a training school for the pilots to be trained to fly these Meteor jet fighters. All we had to do was to to look after the guns and see that they were cleaned and oiled and maintained.

There were two pubs in the village nearby. The officers and the tutors would go in one and all us lot would go in the other. We were quite often joined by the WAAFs who worked in the cookhouse, and my mate and I got friendly with a couple of them. On our way back to the base we would all link arms and go back singing. When we got back and if we were lucky and the girls knew the cook on duty that night, we would get supper as well. It snowed quite a lot and we had to get out and sweep the runway clear so the aircraft could take off and, of course, as soon as we did that it would snow again. Happy days. It was a nice camp, a proper camp with proper buildings and beds and showers and a NAAFI.

We had to undergo training there. The Hurricanes and Spitfires that I was used to had Browning 303s but these new planes had 20 millimetre cannons and I had never seen one of those before. We stripped them down and learned how to maintain them and it was very interesting, We did get quite a lot of weekend leave and I would go down to Edgware to see Una. We would go out and go to the cinema or a cafe: we didn't have restaurants. All you could get was beans on toast or something similar. I had a couple of weeks' leave and we went down to my gran in Faversham. One day we had a walk out into the country and we passed a little old church. The doors were open and we had a look around inside and I popped the question and asked Una if she would marry me.

From Colerne I was posted to Wymondham in Norfolk which I soon found out was called Wyndham. Our duties then were next to nothing by that time as the war was coming to an end. Any enemy bombing really only affected the south, and the squadrons down there dealt with that. I was sent to Woodbridge in Suffolk. We were in Nissen huts there. There was not much to do other than keep the place clean. We were issued with bicycles to cycle to the base and to our billets and of course we cycled out into the country with them. Sometimes at night if some of the lads had been out drinking and came back the worse for wear on their bicycles, singing and shouting, some of the lads in the billet would open the doors at each end of the Nissen huts, and being the worse for wear they would cycle right through and disappear out through the other door and into the distance.

We would cycle to Norwich station at the weekends when we had weekend passes, leave the bikes there and get the train to London. If we were a bit broke we would hitch a lift. One day my mate and I were hitching a lift and this dilapidated car stopped and picked us up. I have never travelled in anything like it, it was an open-topped tourer and looked a complete wreck. When he stopped at a petrol station the attendant filled it up and then the driver got a bottle of something from the boot and tipped that in the petrol tank as well. 'That will make it go faster,' he said. He drove off and drove like some mad demon. He dropped us off at Chelmsford where a cement lorry gave us a lift the rest of the way. We were smothered in cement dust. We were there when the European war came to an end.

I would go down to London to see Una if I had a weekend pass and if Una was also off. I would save up my sweet ration to give to Una and I used to tease her that it was my sweet ration that she was after, not me. Many a time I spent a couple of hours or so waiting for her at the hospital

Harold and Una on their wedding day, 24ᵗʰ October 1945.

gate, because if something happened on the ward the nurses had to stay to sort it out. If somebody died on the ward before she went off duty she would have to stay and lay them out. It was a military hospital and if I was waiting at the gate all the patients would try and embarrass me by waving and blowing kisses at the window.

Una and I arranged our wedding for 24ᵗʰ October 1945. I was at Woodbridge at that time. We went down to the Anchor and Hope near Southampton for our honeymoon. We were a bit bashful and shy and we thought we had got all the confetti out of our clothes but the next morning we were still finding it everywhere. It was a lovely little hotel and we had a lively little honeymoon. Una had a couple of extra days' holiday so I phoned the camp and got my leave extended a couple more days

A long way from Burma. Harold and Una
and their son John, summer 1947.

but the hotel had already got another booking but they could offer us a room at the top of the hotel but it only had a single bed. Well, being on honeymoon we didn't mind, did we. Una got up in the middle of the night and then I found something wet on my face. Una had found the hotel's spaniel dog on the landing and had made a fuss of it and it had followed her back into our room and had licked my face.

I was demobbed in 1946 and was issued with a civilian suit and hat and we all looked alike. The Japanese war had not long ended.

We managed to get a place in Belvedere. It was impossible to get a house at that time as houses were in short supply and you had to have lived in area for a certain amount of time before you could even go on a list. The man who owned the house was a distant relative to one of Una's aunts and he had lost his wife during the war. We had a couple of rooms to ourselves. It wasn't ideal and he expected us to live in with him, so we would quite often go to bed early so we could have a natter and some time to ourselves.

Una became pregnant in 1946 and John was born April 1947. Una was not well during her pregnancy and before John was born she spent a couple of months with her parents in Billericay. At the weekends I would get the train from Belvedere to Tilbury, cross on the ferry and then get a bus to Billericay, and I was doing that every weekend.

I had managed to get a job with Callendar's Cables but it wasn't a very nice job and the conditions were awful. The air in the factory was thick and you could see the metal particles hanging in the air. Where I worked there was a glass roof and in the summer it was unbearably hot and I would sweat through all my clothes and everything looked as though it was covered in rust, even my vests.

I decided we would have a couple of weeks' holiday. John was just a few months old. In those days you only had one week's paid holiday; if you wanted another week you could have it without pay. We went down to Whitstable and found a letter waiting for us from Una's mother. She told us that they had found a bungalow in Pitsea and if we went there we could go and see it. Needless to say we were over the moon. We packed up and went to Billericay, so we only had a day at Whitstable. When we got to Billericay they took us over to Pitsea to see the bungalow and we were over the moon when we saw it and decided to take it there and then. (Una's father bought the bungalow and we paid him rent. After a while he suggested that we got a mortgage for the bungalow and he would accept the rent we had paid him as a deposit. So that was how we became proud house owners.)

I went to see the manager at Callendar's Cables and told him what we were doing and I was told that as I was moving out of the area completely my second week's holiday would be paid for out of my first week's wages, which they would normally hang on to until I left.

I went to the Labour Exchange which was in Hornchurch. I was offered a job working as a labourer on the railway which I turned down, but I was offered a job in the carpenter's shop as Carpenter Grade 2. On one occasion my mate and I were working on a signal box at Hadleigh making new steps up to the box. There were some big horses out in the field that belonged to a farm run by the Salvation Army. When we got there in the morning the horses would be roaming around together, but this particular morning we saw one of the horses standing on its own. None of the other horses were about. Come dinnertime we saw he was still standing in the same position. He hadn't moved so we plucked up courage and went over to him and we found he had caught up his leg in the wire fence and one strand of wire had wrapped itself round the horse's hind leg. Although it had not actually cut into the flesh, where the horse had pulled at it, it was biting right into the leg and must have been very painful. My mate and I had a discussion what to do and we decided that we must try and get the wire off. So we plucked up our courage and entered the field. My mate held the horse's head and I tried to get the wire off the leg. It must have taken us at least half an hour to get it off and the horse never moved. But then the most amazing thing happened. He galloped off a short distance, stopped, and then looked round at us and neighed as though thanking us. He then galloped off and joined the other horses.

The level crossings were made of wood and at Leigh Crossing the gate had collapsed. The gates were massive and the post holes were about 6 foot square.

This particular night it was snowing and there was flood water coming down and we were both saturated. We finished it and it must have been the last train we caught back home to Pitsea. Two of the lads ended up with pneumonia.

Another time we were working at night repairing a crossing. We had to work at night as there were then no trains using the track and one of the lads broke the water main and a jet of water about 10 foot high shot into the air and the water company had to come and repair it before we could finish our job. We started work about seven on the Saturday evening and did not get home until about seven the next evening. Poor Una was up the wall when I got home as there were no phones, no mobiles those days, and she had no idea what had happened.

One day I was sent to Tilbury Docks with a couple of other carpenters and we had to make fenders for the ferry. These were posts which were attached to the side of the quay when the ship was berthing and they would be broken frequently as the ships hit the wall. We would have about five timbers about 10 to 15 foot long, 12 by 12 inches, and we would have to bolt about five together and this would

Family group in the 1950s. Back row l-r aunt Edie, Una, Harold, aunt Lill, Iris wife of cousin Peter, cousin Daphne, cousin Peter, Uncle Bert. Front row l-r aunt Gladys, Granny Bootes, son John.

be done by hand. Then on a Sunday we would put these timbers on rollers and tip them over the edge and fix them. Then one day we were given some different timber called greenheart. All the shavings we would normally sweep into the river and the tide would take them away. However, with this greenheart I noticed that the shavings sunk. On the Sunday the governor came down to supervise what we were doing. He told us to tip the fender over the side and then fix it. We told him it wouldn't float and he told us that it would sink to a level and then it would float and told us to tip it over the edge. It sank like a stone and we never saw it again.

I think that over the years I have walked every bit of

that line from Fenchurch Street to Shoeburyness and round the Tilbury line. Eventually I got a transfer to the Tilbury Ferries. I used to do maintenance on the ferries. If it was a big job then the ferry would have to go to Poplar Dock in London and we would have to travel with it to make sure the job was done properly. I was there for a few years and enjoyed my job when management decided to get new ferries, diesel ferries, and that the workshops at Tilbury would be closed down, so I went back to Upminster where I was put in charge of a gang of labourers. Our job was to maintain the level crossings, mostly farm crossings, renewing the wooden posts with concrete posts and the wooden gates with iron gates and my job was to make sure they were upright and correctly positioned. Eventually it was decided to close Upminster and I got a job with the Council in Basildon which was good. We would would measure up carpentry jobs and take them back to the workshops and make them up into window frames and doors and so on. Then we were given a job of renovating various properties the council had acquired. A lot of them out in the wilds did not have bathrooms and things like that. I was near enough then to being my own governor. Some of the properties would be way out and we would have to turn a room into a bathroom or replace rotten flooring and I enjoyed doing that.

We did anything to do with wood. I had to go out one day to rescue a lady who had got herself locked in a lavatory, and one day I had to go out with the Police to where a man had died in the house. I had to break in for the Police. A lot of variety of jobs came my way and it was all enjoyable.

I was told I could retire at 63 which I did as it meant I could spend all my time with Una. After Una had died I found a little notebook where she had written, 'I have heard today that Harold has been told he can retire early. How lovely. We can now spend the rest of our lives together.' I am glad I did retire early as then we had seven years together. I didn't go to work. I used to help with the housework and we went out shopping every day. It was lovely. When John was divorced he and Samantha would come round Sundays for Sunday dinner. Samantha was getting to be a big girl by then.

We heard that there was going to be a large flyover built at Pitsea which might affect us so we sold up and moved to Basildon, but Una didn't like it. We were there a few years. It was handy for me as it was just a short walk to my work.

Una's mother was starting to go senile at this time. She would burn saucepans by putting things on to cook and forgetting them. She burnt out kettles. She used to poke the gas fire with a knife thinking it was the old coal fire and she would throw paper on it. One day her neighbour came running down to us as she thought she had set the bungalow on fire as there was smoke coming out of it. I rushed down there the bungalow was full of smoke and Una's mother was just sitting there on the settee. Another neighbour had gone in thinking the place was on fire and ended up in hospital as he had chest problems and the smoke got down onto his lungs. She was a big worry. She eventually had to go into hospital and Una and her sister used to go and visit her, but eventually she didn't know who they were. I was sad when

Harold in later life with a group of cousins and son John.

she died as she was a good mother-in-law to me.

Una's father had died some time before. He had been doing some repairs to a roof and fallen and broken his leg, which is not too serious, but he developed a blood clot which moved to his heart. That was a sad time. He was a very nice man. Even though he did threaten to kill me if I upset his daughter.

We moved to Wickford in February 1982. I was still working then but a young lad that I worked with lived in Wickford and he gave me a lift so I was very fortunate.

John now lives in Rettenden Common in a very nice house. On one of our birthdays John took us to Ibiza for a special treat. Much to our amazement Una loved the flight in spite of never having flown before and she hated cars. When we came home we had to get on a little bus to go to the car park she said, 'Ooh, I don't like this,' so she surprised us all.

We had a happy life here after I retired. In 1992 Una fell backwards and hit her head on the kitchen floor and was taken to the hospital unconscious, and since that time she never had good health. During that time Samantha went into hospital to have Bradley so Una was able to give her great-grandson some cuddles before she died.

I had two lovely ladies in my life, my mother and Una, my wife.